It's Never Too Late to LEAD

Discover Your Style, Develop Your Influence,

and Deploy the Leader You Were Always Meant to Be

SHAINE HOBDY

International Award-Winning Author • Leadership Coach •

Experience Strategist

Built on the ALIGN Coaching Model & the FLEX Leadership System

coachtoalign.com | flexforteens.com | theflexleader.com

The ALIGN Coaching Model™ and the FLEX Leadership System™ are trademarks of Shaine Hobdy and SHAINE LLC

Paperback ISBN: 9798257703676

Hardcover ISBN: 9798257711411

For every person who ever looked in the mirror and asked,

"Is it too late for me?"

It isn't.

It never was.

Contents

A Note Before You Begin 7

How to Read This Book 9

MOVEMENT ONE: DISCOVER - Who You Already Are 11

INTRODUCTION..12

What Is a Leader, Really? 25

Meet Your FLEX Personality Style 35

The ALIGN Coaching Model.. 47

Strengths Are Your Starting Line 59

MOVEMENT TWO: DEVELOP -Build the Leader You're Becoming.. 69

Find 70

Learn 79

Empathize 89

eXpand 98

Leading Across Styles 106

MOVEMENT THREE: DEPLOY - Make Your Mark...... 114

Leading in Real Life 115

When Leadership Gets Hard 124

Your Leadership Legacy Starts Now....................................133

IT'S NEVER TOO LATE TO LEAD: CONCLUSION........ 141

APPENDIX A: The FLEX Personality Style Assessment 151

APPENDIX B: Chapter Journaling Prompts 157

APPENDIX C: ALIGN Coaching Worksheets.......................... 161

APPENDIX D: Find Step - Four Dimensions 171

APPENDIX E: Learn – The Learning Loop............................175

APPENDIX F: Empathize – Empathetic Leadership 180

APPENDIX G: eXpand – Expansion Growth Zone 181

ACKNOWLEDGMENTS: With Gratitude...................................182

Shaine Hobdy

A Note Before You Begin

The book you are holding is not a leadership book for leaders. It is a leadership book for people, for anyone who has ever felt that the noise, the pressure, the expectations, and the mythology surrounding leadership were designed for someone else.

Shaine Hobdy has spent four decades working in environments where leadership was not optional: where the standard was excellence, the stakes were real, and the people who rose were not always the ones with the most impressive titles but the ones with the most authentic self-knowledge and the most genuine commitment to the people around them. This book is the distillation of those four decades, filtered through a framework that is rigorous without being clinical, practical without being simplistic, and personal in the way that only experience-earned wisdom can be.

What you will find in these pages is not a collection of best practices borrowed from other authors and repackaged with new names. The FLEX Leadership System framework and the ALIGN Coaching Model are Shaine's own intellectual contributions, built from scratch in the laboratory of real leadership in real organizations with real human beings whose development depended on the quality of the frameworks being applied.

Read this book with a pen. The margins are for your thinking. The reflection questions are not rhetorical. The worksheets are not decorative. This is a working document. Treat it as one. The leader you are becoming deserves that level of engagement.

Shaine Hobdy

How to Read This Book

This book is designed to be read in order. The movements build on each other: you need DISCOVER before DEVELOP makes full sense and DEVELOP before DEPLOY has its greatest impact. That said, if you are a leader with specific and urgent challenges, you may find it useful to read targeted chapters first and then return to the full sequence.

A word about real-world examples throughout the book. All the individuals referenced in composite examples are fictionalized composites of real leadership situations. Any resemblance to a specific individual is coincidental. The situations are real. The specific people are not identifiable.

The FLEX Leadership System and the ALIGN Coaching Model are designed to be useful across a wide range of cultural, generational, and professional contexts. Leadership is not a culturally neutral practice, and I want to acknowledge that the frameworks in this book were developed and tested primarily in North American professional contexts. They will translate across cultures, but they will require contextual adaptation. Your cultural lens is not a deviation from the frameworks. It is a necessary and valuable part of how you apply them.

Finally, a note on language. Throughout this book I use the term "leader" expansively and the word "team" broadly. A team might be a group of colleagues, a classroom of students, a family, a community group, or any configuration of people whose development you have some responsibility to. If your current context does not look like a traditional organizational team, read "team" as the people in your sphere of influence. The concepts apply regardless.

Now: take a breath. You are about to begin the most important leadership development work you will ever do, because it is about you.

MOVEMENT ONE: DISCOVER - Who You Already Are

The work of DISCOVER is the work of honest seeing. Before you can lead any person, any team, any cause, or any organization toward anything worth going toward, you must know yourself with a clarity that does not flinch from what it finds. Movement One gives you the framework and the language for that kind of clear-eyed self-knowledge.

In the chapters ahead, you will learn what leadership really is and dismantle the myths that have kept you from claiming it. You will discover your FLEX personality style and understand how your natural wiring shapes everything about how you lead. You will be introduced to the ALIGN Coaching Model that will serve as your development blueprint for the entire journey of this book. And you will begin to claim, without apology, the genuine strengths that are your leadership starting line.

Begin with curiosity. Resist the temptation to read quickly. The work of DISCOVER rewards the ones who are willing to sit with it.

IT'S NEVER TOO LATE TO LEAD

INTRODUCTION

The Moment Everything Changes

Close your eyes for a moment.

Actually, don't. You're reading a book. But take a breath and stay with me for the next sixty seconds, because what I'm about to say is the most important thing anyone in the field of leadership has ever not said to you.

You are already a leader.

Not in the someday version of that sentence. Not in the "when-you-get-the-promotion" version. Not in the "when-you-finally-feel-ready" version. Right now. Today. In the life you are actually living, in the relationships you are already in, in the moments that are already happening around you, you are a leader. And somewhere along the way, someone — or a hundred someone's — convinced you otherwise.

This book is the beginning of your refusal to believe that lie any longer.

The Voice in the Room

I want to tell you about a particular voice. You have heard it. You know it. You may have mistaken it for reason, for humility, for realism.

It is the voice that says: *"That's not really my place."*

It is the voice that says: *"Someone else would be better at this."*

It is the voice that says: *"I'll step up when I'm more experienced."* Or more educated. Or more confident. Or just… more.

It is the voice that says, quietly but persistently, in the back of a classroom when you have the right answer and do not raise your hand, in the middle of a meeting when you see the solution no one else has noticed, in the middle of the night when the version of yourself you most want to become feels impossibly far from the version you are right now: *"Is it too late for me?"*

I know that voice. I have heard it in the mouths of eighteen-year-olds starting their first job and fifty-eight-year-olds stepping into leadership roles for the first time. I have heard it from corporate directors who have spent decades leading hundreds of people and still doubt their right to be in the room. I have heard it from parents, from students, from community volunteers, from coaches and teachers and first-generation professionals who carry remarkable gifts and cannot seem to believe those gifts are enough.

That voice is not the truth. That voice is the absence of a framework. And this book is the framework.

> *The world does not lack leaders. It lacks people who have been given the tools to recognize that they already are one. – Shaine Hobdy, Author*

Who This Book Is For

Let me be specific about who I wrote this for, because the most powerful books are the ones that make you feel, from the very first page, that the author already knows you.

This book is for the sixteen-year-old who is navigating a social landscape that feels like a full-time leadership course no one signed them up for, who has more insight than they have been given credit for and more influence than they know how to name.

This book is for the twenty-six-year-old who is three years into a career and realizes that the version of leadership they imagined in college looks nothing like what is actually required of them in the real world, and who is trying to figure out who they actually are as a leader rather than who they thought they were supposed to be.

This book is for the forty-three-year-old who has been quietly leading for two decades without the title, the recognition, or the framework to understand the depth of what they have been doing, and who is finally ready to lead with intention instead of instinct alone.

This book is for the sixty-year-old who has watched leadership trends cycle through their organization like fashions, who has outlasted management fads and leadership gurus and restructuring initiatives, and who wants, finally, a framework built on something more durable than whatever was trending last year.

It is for the student and the executive. The parent and the peer mentor. The person who has been told their style is wrong and the person who has been told they are not ready and the person who has simply been too afraid to believe they are enough.

You are enough. And this book is going to prove it to you, specifically, practically, and without a single moment of empty inspiration.

The Problem Nobody Is Talking About Honestly

Here is the real leadership crisis, and it is not the one that makes the covers of business magazines.

The crisis is not a shortage of leadership books. There are more of those than you could read in a lifetime. It is not a shortage of leadership advice. Every platform, every podcast, every conference, every mentor with a business card is full of it.

The crisis is that the vast majority of people with genuine leadership capacity are walking through their lives completely unable to see it. Not because they are unaware. Because they have been given a definition of leadership that does not include them.

The definition they inherited looks like this: Leadership is for people with authority. Leadership is for the loudest, most confident, most traditionally impressive person in the room. Leadership happens at the top. Leadership requires a title, a team, a track record, a particular way of speaking, a particular way of looking, a particular way of being that either fits you or does not.

That definition is not just incomplete. It is actively harmful. It has kept generations of capable, visionary, empathetic, disciplined, creative, and deeply needed leaders on the sidelines of their own potential, waiting for a permission that was never coming because it was never theirs to wait for.

The permission was always theirs to give themselves.

And that is where this book begins.

> *Leadership is not a credential you earn. It is a decision you make. And the most powerful thing I can tell you is this: you can make it today. — Shaine Hobdy, Author*

What Is Actually Wrong With Most Leadership Books

I want to take thirty seconds to do something unusual: be honest about the category of book you are holding.

Most leadership books are written for a specific type of person and that person has already arrived. They already have the title. They already have the team. They already have the platform. The book is designed to help them optimize what they have, and it does that well. But if you are still building toward that kind of position, or if you are leading in contexts that do not look like a corporate org chart, those books leave you with a peculiar combination of inspiration and irrelevance. You feel motivated and simultaneously unseen.

Other leadership books swing to the opposite extreme. They are written so broadly, aimed at everyone from teenagers to retirees, that they become so general as to be nearly useless. They give you universal principles that sound right and feel right and produce no specific change because they are not connected to who you specifically are and what you specifically need to develop.

And then there is the third category: books that are essentially personality assessments dressed as leadership guides. They give you a label and leave you there. You discover that you are an introvert or an analytical or a Type A and you think, Yes, that's me, and then you close the book having learned what you already suspected and having gained no additional capacity to lead.

This book is none of those things.

It begins with self-discovery because self-knowledge is the indispensable foundation of any leadership that lasts. But it does not stop there. It connects your specific personality wiring, your FLEX Leadership Style, to a specific developmental framework, the ALIGN Coaching Model, and then walks you, step by step, through the practical application of both in the real contexts of your actual life. It is a system. A coherent, tested, real-world system that has been refined across four decades of leadership practice in some of the most demanding organizational environments in the world: Walt Disney World, Ritz-Carlton Hotels, Park Hyatt Hotels, United Airlines, jetBlue, Asurion, and Assurant.

This is not theory dressed in the language of practice. This is practice. And it is yours now.

The FLEX Leadership System and the ALIGN Coaching Model: A Quick Map

Before we go any further, you deserve to know what tools you are about to be given.

The FLEX Leadership System framework identifies four distinct leadership personality styles: the Feeler, who leads through deep relational intelligence and genuine empathy; the Thinker, who leads through analytical precision and rigorous decision-making; the Controller, who leads through decisive action and high accountability; and the Entertainer, who leads through visionary energy and inspirational communication.

Every person has a dominant FLEX Personality style. That style is not a box you are being placed in. It is a mirror being held up so that, possibly for the first time, you can see clearly what you are already doing when you lead at your best, why you create certain kinds of friction when you lead at your default, and how you can expand your range to become more effective with more people in more situations.

The ALIGN Coaching Model is the five-dimension developmental framework that sits beneath the FLEX Personality styles and gives them direction. ALIGN stands for Analyze Behaviors, Leverage Relationships, Inquire, Gain Next Steps, and New Commitment. Together, these five steps form a structured coaching conversation framework that transforms everyday leadership interactions into genuine turning points. They are not theory. They are a disciplined sequence proven across four decades of real-world leadership practice.

And woven through the entire second movement of the book is the FLEX formula: Find, Learn, Empathize, eXpand. These four steps are the operational engine of your growth, the practical daily practice that turns self-knowledge into leadership capacity.

You will understand all of this completely before you reach the end of Chapter Three. I am offering it now not as instruction but as reassurance: this book has a spine. It is coherent. Every piece is connected. You are not being asked to collect a handful of interesting ideas. You are being asked to build something.

The Transformation This Book Delivers

Let me be direct about what will be different when you finish this book, if you engage it honestly.

You will know your leadership style with a precision that allows you to stop wasting energy trying to be a different kind of leader and start investing that energy in becoming the most fully developed version of the leader you actually are.

You will have a personal leadership blueprint, built on the ALIGN Coaching Model, that is specific to your wiring, your context, and your goals. Not a generic plan. Yours.

You will have a four-step formula for continuous growth that makes every experience, every setback, every success, and every relationship in your leadership life a source of compounding development rather than simply accumulated time.

You will understand how to lead across different personality styles with a fluency that will change the quality of your most important professional and personal relationships.

You will have confronted the hard parts: failure, doubt, imposter syndrome, resilience, and the question of whether any of it matters, and you will have found, in the honest engagement of those questions, that it does.

And you will have begun building your legacy. Not at the end of a career. Now. Because the leader you are becoming is already making a difference to someone who is watching, and that difference compounds with every day you choose to lead with intention.

THE PROMISE OF THIS BOOK

When you finish this book, you will not be a different person. You will be a more fully realized version of the person you already are. You will see yourself more clearly, lead others more effectively, and carry the unshakeable knowledge that the leadership you were always meant to practice is not something you have to earn. It is something you were already carrying. This book is how you learn to use it.

A Word About 'Too Late'

I want to spend one final moment with the title of this book, because it is not accidental, and I do not want it to pass without being fully seen.

The phrase "It's Never Too Late" carries two distinct and equally important meanings.

The first meaning is for the person who feels like they are starting over, who is coming to leadership development later than they imagined, who has watched others get further ahead and is quietly convinced that the gap is now too large to close. For that person, this phrase is a direct answer: it is not too late. The compound growth that comes from even five years of intentional, framework-driven leadership development is more significant than most people believe. The starting point is not an indictment. It is just a coordinate.

The second meaning is for the person who already has experience, who has been leading for years, and who has developed habits, patterns, and assumptions that have never been examined in the clear light of a coherent framework. For that person, "it's never too late" means something different: it is not too late to change what is not working. It is not too late to develop the growth edge you have been avoiding for fifteen years. It is not too late to lead with the authenticity and intention that your experience always deserved but your lack of self-knowledge prevented.

For both people, and for everyone between them, this book is the same answer to the same underlying question: ***Is the best of my leadership still ahead of me?***

Yes. Unequivocally. Probably. Yes.

Now turn the page.

Everything that follows is yours.

CHAPTER ONE

What Is a Leader, Really?
Redefining Leadership for Every Age

"Leadership is not about being in charge. It is about taking care of those in your charge."
— Simon Sinek

Ask ten people to define leadership and you will get eleven different answers. Some will say it is about authority: the person at the top of the org chart who makes the decisions. Others will say it is about charisma: the magnetic personality who commands attention the moment they walk into a room. Some will point to history: generals, presidents, CEOs, activists. A few might get philosophical and talk about vision. Fewer still will point to themselves.

That final group, the ones who hesitate to name themselves as leaders, is precisely the group this book is for. Because here is what forty years of observing, practicing, studying, and coaching leadership has taught me: the most common form of leadership failure is not bad leadership. It is invisible leadership. It is the kind that sits in a person's chest, fully formed and deeply capable, never given a name and therefore never given a chance.

Before we can talk about how to develop your leadership, we need to dismantle some of the stories that may have already been written for you. Stories about who leaders are, what they look like, when they are born, and whether you qualify.

The Myths We Have Been Sold

Myth number one: Leaders are born, not made. This is perhaps the most pervasive and damaging idea in leadership culture. It suggests that somewhere in your genetic material, your destiny as a leader was either switched on or off. It implies that some people are simply wired for leadership and others are not, and that the gap between the two groups is unbridgeable.

The research tells a completely different story. Decades of work in developmental psychology, organizational behavior, and neuroscience consistently confirm that while certain personality traits may create natural advantages in some leadership contexts, the core competencies of effective leadership, things like communication, emotional intelligence, strategic thinking, and the ability to inspire others, are all learnable. They are skills, not gifts. And skills can always be built.

Myth number two: Leaders are the loudest people in the room. Somewhere along the way, we conflated volume with vision. We started believing that the person who speaks first and most confidently must be the one worth following. That belief has cost organizations, communities, and teams some of their most thoughtful and effective leadership, because the quietest voice in the room is often carrying the most sophisticated perspective.

Myth number three: Leaders need a title. This one has done incalculable damage. People postpone their leadership, waiting for a promotion that will finally authorize them to act. They say things like, "Once I have a team to manage, I will start leading." Or, "When I get that VP role, then I will show what I can do." Meanwhile, the leadership that was available to them all along, the kind that does not require a business card, goes unpracticed and undeveloped.

Myth number four: Leaders have it all figured out. This myth is particularly cruel because it sets an impossible standard. Real leaders, the ones I have watched transform organizations and lives over four decades, are not people who have everything sorted. They are people who have developed the discipline to act with clarity even in the presence of uncertainty. They make decisions without perfect information, maintain composure without personal certainty, and project confidence that is not the absence of doubt but the management of it.

KEY INSIGHT

Leadership is not the absence of uncertainty. It is the choice to move forward responsibly in spite of it. Every great leader you admire has been afraid. The difference is that they moved anyway.

A New Definition Worth Living By

If those myths are not the truth, what is? Let me offer a definition that I have refined through practice and that will serve as the foundation for everything that follows in this book.

LEADERSHIP DEFINED

Leadership is the consistent practice of knowing yourself deeply, influencing others intentionally, and creating conditions where people and possibilities can flourish, regardless of your title, age, position, or circumstance.

Let's unpack that definition because every word in it matters.

Consistent practice means leadership is not an event. It is not a speech you give or a crisis you navigate or a title you receive. It is what you do every day, in the small moments and the large ones. The leader who remembers a coworker's name after one introduction, who takes the extra minute to acknowledge someone's effort, who prepares more carefully than required not because anyone is watching but because the standard matters, that is consistent practice.

Knowing yourself deeply is the starting point of every leadership journey worth taking. It is what the entire first movement of this book is designed to build. You cannot lead from a place you have never been. You cannot offer others stability if you have never found your own footing. Self-knowledge is not navel-gazing. It is the most practical investment a leader can make.

Influencing others intentionally is where leadership becomes relational. Influence is not manipulation. It is not pressure or persuasion that bypasses someone's autonomy. Intentional influence means you are deliberately, thoughtfully, and ethically working to affect how people think, feel, decide, or act, and you are doing it in service of outcomes that are genuinely good for them.

Creating conditions where people and possibilities can flourish is the generative dimension of leadership. The best leaders I have known did not hoard opportunity. They expanded it. They saw human potential not as competition but as something to be nurtured. They built environments, in teams, in families, in communities, where people became more capable and more confident by being in their presence.

And the final phrase, regardless of your title, age, position, or circumstance, is the one that makes this definition yours. You do not need to earn this definition. You do not need to wait for it. It applies to you now, today, exactly where you are.

Leadership at Every Age

One of the most illuminating exercises I have done in workshops with mixed-age audiences is to ask people to name the most influential leader they have ever personally known. Not a celebrity or a historical figure, but someone in their actual life.

What consistently emerges is extraordinary. A grandmother who never earned a degree but whose kitchen table was where three generations came to solve their hardest problems. A sixteen-year-old who organized her school's first mental health awareness week because she was tired of watching her friends suffer in silence. A thirty-eight-year-old warehouse team lead who had no formal management training but whose section always performed at the top because he treated every person like they mattered, because they did.

None of these people had been waiting for permission. They had simply recognized a need, assessed their ability to address it, and moved. That is leadership in its most essential form, and it does not belong to any age group.

That said, different stages of life offer different leadership laboratories, and it is worth acknowledging them. The teenager navigating peer dynamics in a cafeteria is practicing the same fundamental skills as the executive navigating stakeholder dynamics in a boardroom. The vocabulary changes. The stakes are framed differently. But the core work, understanding people, building trust, communicating with clarity, managing conflict, adapting your approach, is identical.

If you are young, I want you to know this: the leadership habits you build before the world starts paying attention to you are the ones that will carry you the farthest. The discipline of preparation. The practice of listening more than speaking. The commitment to following through when no one is checking. These are not skills you develop at thirty. They are skills you build right now, in the unglamorous everyday moments that most people dismiss as insignificant.

If you are not young, I want you to know this: experience is not a substitute for growth, but it is an extraordinary accelerant of it. Every leadership lesson you have already absorbed, every difficult conversation you have navigated, every team you have held together under pressure, is material. Your age is not a liability. It is a library.

Formal and Informal Leadership

There are two categories of leadership that are worth distinguishing early, because they carry very different social cues and yet require exactly the same internal foundation.

Formal leadership comes with structural authority. It is the manager, the director, the elected official, the head coach. Formal leadership is conferred by others and comes with built-in leverage: people report to you, listen to you in meetings, and defer to your decisions in ways that are procedurally expected. The danger of formal leadership is that it can be confused with actual leadership. Titles can be granted to people who have not developed the internal foundations, and when that happens, the title becomes a costume rather than a credential.

Informal leadership has no structural backing. It earns its influence through demonstrated value, genuine relationship, and consistent trustworthiness. Informal leaders are the people others turn to when something goes wrong, not because they are required to but because they have proven that their perspective, their calm, their competence, is worth seeking out. Informal leadership is often the proving ground for formal leadership, but it does not require formal leadership as its destination. Many of the most impactful informal leaders never take a management role, and the world is better for what they do.

This book will serve you in both categories. The self-knowledge tools and the FLEX Leadership System framework are equally applicable whether you are leading with a title or without one. The ALIGN Coaching Model is as relevant for a student body president as it is for a regional vice president. Good leadership is good leadership, and its roots do not care about your org chart position.

The Leadership Identity

Before we move into the practical frameworks, I want to invite you to sit with one more idea. Leadership is not just something you do. At its fullest expression, it becomes something you are. Not in a grandiose or self-important way, but in the same quiet way that honesty or curiosity becomes a characteristic. It is the orientation you bring to every room, every relationship, every challenge.

Developing a leadership identity means deciding, consciously and explicitly, that you are someone who takes responsibility, who looks for ways to serve, who grows on purpose, and who treats other people's development as a worthy investment of their own time and energy. It is a decision, not a discovery. And like every decision worth making, it can be made today.

In the chapters ahead, you are going to get specific. You are going to name your FLEX personality style, map your ALIGN Coaching Model blueprint, and build a leadership practice that is uniquely, powerfully, and authentically yours. But the work that this chapter has begun, dismantling the myths, claiming a new definition, and accepting that leadership is already inside you, that work is the soil everything else grows in.

Take a moment. Sit with the idea that you are already a leader. Not the leader you will be after reading this book. The leader you already are, right now, with everything you already know and carry and have survived. That leader is the starting point.

Everything that follows is refinement.

REFLECTION QUESTIONS

1.   What has been your personal definition of leadership up to this point? Where did that definition come from?

2.   Which of the four leadership myths has had the most influence on how you see yourself as a leader?

3.   Name one person in your real life who demonstrates informal leadership. What specifically makes them effective?

4.   Write down one sentence that describes the kind of leader you want to be known as.

This area is for your thoughts:

CHAPTER TWO

Meet Your FLEX Personality Style
Feeler, Thinker, Controller, Entertainer

"Knowing yourself is the beginning of all wisdom."
— Aristotle

There is a reason you read some leaders and immediately trust them, while others, equally credentialed and experienced, leave you cold. There is a reason certain meetings energize you and others drain every ounce of motivation you walked in with. There is a reason the feedback that lands for one team member goes straight over the head of another. That reason is not random, and it is not mysterious. It is style.

The FLEX Leadership System Framework was built on a foundational premise: people do not have the same leadership wiring, and no single leadership style is inherently superior to another. What determines effectiveness is not which style you have, but how well you understand it, how honestly you work with it, and how skillfully you adapt it when the situation calls for a different approach.

The FLEX Framework identifies four distinct leadership styles. Each one has a name, a natural orientation, a set of signature strengths, and a set of growth edges. None is perfect. All are necessary. And most people, while they have a dominant style, carry elements of the others. Understanding your primary FLEX personality style is not about boxing yourself in. It is about giving yourself a mirror precise enough to actually be useful.

The Four FLEX Personality Styles: An Overview

Before we explore each style in depth, here is the landscape. The four FLEX personality styles are: the Feeler, the Thinker, the Controller, and the Entertainer. You will likely recognize yourself in more than one, and that is entirely expected. What you are looking for is your dominant orientation, the style that most consistently describes how you naturally show up when leadership is required of you.

As you read the descriptions that follow, resist the temptation to choose the style that sounds most impressive. Choose the one that sounds most like you, including the growth edges. The growth edges are not flaws. They are the specific areas where your style, when unexamined, can create friction. Naming them honestly is the single most effective thing you can do to accelerate your leadership development.

THE FEELER

Leading with heart. Connecting before directing.

The Feeler leads from the emotional center. They are deeply attuned to the people around them, highly relational, and motivated by the quality of the connections they build. Feelers tend to read a room with extraordinary accuracy. They sense tension before it surfaces, notice when someone is disengaged, and instinctively move toward the human dimension of any challenge. In group settings, Feelers are often the ones who check in on colleagues, remember personal details, and create the psychological safety that allows teams to do their best work.

NATURAL STRENGTHS

Building deep trust quickly, creating inclusive environments, navigating interpersonal conflict with compassion, motivating people individually, bringing warmth and humanity to leadership moments that might otherwise feel transactional.

GROWTH EDGES

Difficulty making decisions that will disappoint others, sometimes prioritizing harmony over necessary honesty, taking criticism personally when it was not personal, struggling to maintain boundaries in high-empathy situations, occasionally avoiding conflict that needs to be engaged directly.

THE THINKER

Leading with precision. Analyzing before acting.

The Thinker leads from the analytical center. They are systematic, thorough, and deeply motivated by accuracy. Before a Thinker takes action, they have considered the data, examined the variables, tested the assumptions, and identified the most likely failure points. They are the leaders who ask the questions others did not think to ask and catch the errors others did not think to look for. In organizations, Thinkers are invaluable in strategy development, quality assurance, financial planning, and any situation where getting it right matters more than getting it done fast.

NATURAL STRENGTHS

Exceptional attention to detail, high-quality decision-making under defined parameters, systematic problem-solving, credibility through competence, long-term strategic thinking, and the ability to explain complex ideas with precision.

GROWTH EDGES

Difficulty communicating in informal or emotionally-charged contexts, sometimes paralyzed by the pursuit of perfect information, struggling to build rapid rapport, being perceived as cold or critical even when the intent is rigorous improvement, and missing the big picture when too deep in the details.

THE CONTROLLER

Leading with drive. Deciding before deliberating.

The Controller leads from the goal-oriented center. They are decisive, results-focused, and energized by momentum. Controllers have a remarkable ability to cut through ambiguity and identify the path forward. They are the leaders who thrive in crisis situations, who take ownership when others are still debating options, and who produce results even in conditions that would slow most people down. In organizations, Controllers are often the ones who set the pace, raise the bar, and demand that plans translate into outcomes.

NATURAL STRENGTHS

Rapid decision-making, exceptional ownership and accountability, the ability to execute under pressure, clear communication of expectations, high personal standards that elevate the people around them, and a results orientation that keeps teams focused when distractions multiply.

GROWTH EDGES

Can appear impatient or dismissive of process, sometimes moves too fast for the team to maintain alignment, may undervalue the relational dimensions of leadership, can create environments where people feel more evaluated than supported, and may struggle with delegation because their standards are so high.

THE ENTERTAINER

Leading with energy. Inspiring before implementing.

The Entertainer leads from the inspirational center. They are enthusiastic, visionary, and gifted at generating excitement about what is possible. Entertainers have a rare ability to make other people feel seen, valued, and motivated. They are natural storytellers, skilled communicators, and magnetic presences who often energize whatever room they occupy. In organizations, Entertainers are frequently found at the forefront of culture-building, change management, and brand representation, because their optimism and passion are genuinely contagious.

NATURAL STRENGTHS

Building excitement and buy-in around a vision, making people feel welcomed and appreciated, generating creative energy, navigating change with adaptability, presenting and communicating with impact, and creating organizational cultures where people actually want to show up.

GROWTH EDGES

Can struggle with follow-through once the excitement of an idea fades, may resist routine or structure even when it is needed, can overpromise in the enthusiasm of the moment, may find it difficult to deliver hard feedback, and sometimes prioritizes the energy of the room over the substance of the work.

Reading Your Dominant Style

Now that you have read all four descriptions, you probably have a sense of where you lean. Your dominant FLEX personality style is the one that felt most like reading your own journal: recognizable, a little uncomfortable in the growth edges section, and accurate enough to sting just slightly.

Here is something important to hold onto: your dominant style is not your only style. All four styles exist on a spectrum, and most people operate with a primary style and one or two secondary influences. A Feeler might have strong Thinker tendencies that show up in high-stakes decision-making. An Entertainer might shift into Controller mode when a deadline is looming. A Controller might have Feeler undercurrents that explain why their team is fiercely loyal to them even though they run a tight ship.

What the FLEX Leadership System framework is asking you to do is not to choose a permanent category. It is to develop honest awareness of your default orientation, the setting you return to under pressure, in unfamiliar situations, when you are tired or stressed or operating on instinct. That default is where your leadership either serves you brilliantly or creates its most predictable friction.

Complete the full FLEX Personality Assessment in Appendix A to confirm your dominant style with precision. But for now, trust your instinct. The style that felt most accurate as you read through the descriptions is probably your answer. The brain recognizes patterns it already lives in.

Why Style Matters in Leadership

You might be wondering why we are spending an entire chapter on personality styles when there is so much else to learn about leadership. Here is why: everything else you learn about leadership will be filtered through your style. Your communication, your decision-making process, your conflict approach, how you motivate others and how you yourself are motivated, all of it is style-influenced. If you do not understand your style, you cannot understand your leadership.

I watched this play out in a vivid way during my years in the hospitality industry. I worked alongside leaders who were genuinely talented but chronically ineffective, and in almost every case, the root cause was a gap between their natural style and the way they were trying to lead. A natural Thinker trying to lead like a charismatic Entertainer because they believed that was what leadership looked like. A gifted Feeler who was suppressing their relational instincts because they had been told that real leaders do not get emotional. The mismatch was exhausting and the results were poor.

Conversely, some of the most quietly extraordinary leaders I have encountered were people who understood exactly who they were and leaned into it with precision. A Thinker-dominant Director at a major airline who ran the most error-free operations I had ever seen, not because she was inspiring or charismatic, but because her natural analytical rigor created systems so sound that the entire team performed at a higher level simply by operating within them. A Feeler-dominant team lead at a luxury hotel property whose guest satisfaction scores were consistently the highest in the region, not because he was the most experienced, but because every single guest felt that he actually cared about them, because he did.

Your style, understood and applied with intention, is your most durable leadership asset. Developed and refined over a lifetime, it becomes your leadership signature.

No Hierarchy, No Competition

This point is important enough to repeat: no FLEX personality style is superior to another. Organizations need all four. Communities need all four. Teams need all four. The best leadership in any context comes not from one dominant style overruling the others but from a diversity of styles working in informed collaboration.

What creates problems is not having a particular style. What creates problems is not knowing your style, being unwilling to develop your growth edges, or dismissing the contributions of people whose style is different from yours. A Controller who cannot value the Feeler's relational intelligence will build teams that perform in the short term and fracture in the long term. An Entertainer who never incorporates the Thinker's precision will generate excitement that fails to land because the execution was not thought through. A Feeler who cannot embrace the Controller's directness will lead teams that are emotionally safe but strategically adrift.

Every style has something to offer. Every style has something to learn. That mutual dependency is not a design flaw. It is the point. Leadership development is not about becoming more like your opposite style. It is about becoming fluent enough in the full FLEX personality range that you can collaborate across differences, adapt your approach to the situation, and draw on the strengths of people whose natural wiring complements yours.

The FLEX Formula: <u>F</u>ind, <u>L</u>earn, <u>E</u>mpathize, e<u>X</u>pand

The FLEX acronym does double duty in this framework. FLEX is both the name for the four personality styles and the name for the four-step leadership formula that drives your development across those styles.

Find means locating yourself with honest precision. Where are you right now in your leadership? What is working? What is creating friction? What are you avoiding that you know you need to face? Finding requires self-assessment without self-deception, and it is the foundation of everything that follows.

Learn means treating every experience, including and especially the difficult ones, as a source of growth data. Leaders who learn continuously compound their effectiveness over time in a way that leaders who simply accumulate experience never do. Experience is not wisdom. Experience plus reflection plus application equals wisdom.

Empathize means developing the capacity to understand and respond to the inner life of the people you lead. Empathy is not agreement. It is not emotional merger. It is the disciplined practice of seeing the world from another person's perspective clearly enough to lead them with genuine relevance.

eXpand means deliberately moving beyond your default zone. It means taking on the challenge, the role, the conversation, the opportunity that you would have declined at an earlier version of yourself. eXpand is the mechanism of growth that all the previous steps are building toward. Without it, discovery and learning and empathy remain theoretical.

You will spend four full chapters in Movement Two walking through each step of this formula. For now, simply notice that the formula begins where all good things begin: with knowing who and where you are.

REFLECTION QUESTIONS

1.   Which FLEX personality style felt most like your natural default? What specific detail convinced you?

2.   Which of your dominant style's growth edges do you most recognize in yourself right now?

3.   Think of a leader you have admired. What FLEX personality style do you think they operated from primarily?

4.   How might your style be creating unintentional friction in a current relationship or role? What would you change if you understood your style better?

This area is for your thoughts:

CHAPTER THREE

The ALIGN Coaching Model
Your Personal Leadership Blueprint

> *"The quality of your questions determines the quality of your life."*
> — Tony Robbins

Most leadership conversations stay on the surface. They talk about what happened, who did what, and what the numbers say. They rarely go deeper, into why a behavior keeps recurring, what is really driving a team member's disengagement, or what a leader needs to stop doing, start doing, or do differently to produce a different result. Surface conversations produce surface change. The ALIGN Coaching Model was built to go deeper.

The ALIGN Coaching Model is a five-step framework for structured, high-impact leadership conversations. It is the methodology I developed and refined across four decades of leadership practice in some of the most demanding service environments in the world. Whether I was coaching a frontline team member at a Ritz-Carlton property, developing a supervisor at Asurion, or working with a senior leader at Assurant navigating a complex transformation, the ALIGN

Coaching Model provided the structure that turned ordinary feedback conversations into genuine turning points.

The word ALIGN is not accidental. Every leadership challenge I have ever observed, at every level of every organization, has at its root a misalignment: between behavior and expectation, between potential and performance, between the leader a person wants to be and the habits they are actually practicing. ALIGN gives you a systematic way to find that misalignment, name it with specificity, explore it with curiosity, and resolve it with commitment.

The Five Steps of the ALIGN Coaching Model

ALIGN stands for <u>A</u>nalyze Behaviors, <u>L</u>everage Relationships, <u>I</u>nquire, <u>G</u>ain Next Steps, and <u>N</u>ew Commitment. Each step builds on the one before it, creating a conversational arc that moves from observation through understanding to action. These are not rigid scripts. They are a disciplined sequence that ensures you never skip the step that most conversations miss and that most leadership failures trace back to.

A — Analyze Behaviors

The first step is the one most leaders skip in their rush to provide feedback: the Analyze step. Before you say anything, you observe everything. You gather data from multiple sources, direct observation, performance metrics, peer feedback, customer input, and team dynamics, to build a comprehensive and accurate picture of what is actually happening with a team member or within yourself as a leader.

Analyzing behaviors means looking for patterns, not isolated incidents. A single missed deadline is an event. Consistently missing deadlines on Monday mornings is a pattern, and patterns have causes. The leader who jumps immediately to the feedback conversation without first doing the analytical work will address the symptom and miss the cause. The result is a conversation that feels comprehensive but produces no lasting change.

When you apply the Analyze step to your own leadership, the practice becomes a form of rigorous self-examination. You are gathering data about your own behavioral patterns: where your FLEX style is serving you, where it is creating friction you did not intend, and where the gap between how you see yourself as a leader and how your team experiences you is larger than you realized. This kind of honest analysis is uncomfortable. It is also the most accurate map of your actual leadership that you will ever have.

The FLEX Leadership System framework is an essential tool in the Analyze step. When you understand your dominant FLEX personality style and the styles of the people around you, you have a lens for interpreting the behavioral data you are gathering. A Controller's tendency to move quickly past the emotional dimensions of a situation is not a character flaw. It is a behavioral pattern rooted in style, and it has a predictable impact on the people around them. Analyzing that pattern is the first step toward addressing it.

L — Leverage Relationships

Data without relationship produces defensiveness. This is one of the most important insights in all of leadership development, and it is what the Leverage Relationships step is designed to prevent. Before you can have a productive, honest, growth-oriented conversation with someone, you need to have built enough trust with that person that they will be open to hearing what you have to say.

Leveraging Relationships means investing in the human connection before the professional conversation. It means knowing the people you lead as individuals: their aspirations, their pressures, their communication preferences, their history with feedback, and the experiences that have shaped their professional identity. This knowledge does not happen in the moment of a formal review. It is built through consistent, genuine engagement over time, informal check-ins, real conversations, and the simple but powerful act of showing up for people in the small moments that shape whether they trust you.

When trust exists, feedback lands differently. The same honest observation that would create defensiveness in a low-trust relationship can produce genuine reflection and commitment to change in a high-trust one. The difference is not the content of the feedback. It is the relationship through which the feedback travels. Leaders who invest in Leveraging

Relationships find that their coaching conversations are more efficient, more honest, and more likely to produce lasting behavioral change than the conversations of leaders who skip this step.

For the person reading this book who is still building their leadership track record, the Leverage Relationships step is where your FLEX personality strengths become your most valuable asset. The Feeler's natural warmth, the Entertainer's ability to make people feel valued, even the Thinker's genuine interest in the details of someone's work, all of these are relationship-building assets when they are deployed with intentionality and consistency.

I — Inquire

The Inquire step is where the ALIGN Coaching Model most distinguishes itself from traditional feedback frameworks. Rather than telling a person what you have observed and directing them toward a predetermined solution, the Inquire step asks them powerful questions that help them discover the root cause of their own behavior. This distinction is not cosmetic. It is the difference between compliance and genuine commitment.

Inquiry uses a structured question framework built around five dimensions: Who, What, Where, When, and Why. Together, these questions create a comprehensive picture of the situation from the inside out. Who is involved and who might be influencing the behavior? What specifically happened, and what was the outcome? Where and when does the pattern occur, and are there conditions that trigger it? And most critically, Why? Why did this behavior emerge, and what is the root cause underneath the surface explanation?

The Why question is where the real work happens. In my experience across four decades of leadership conversations, the first answer a person gives to "Why?" is almost never the real answer. It is usually the most socially acceptable explanation, the one that protects their ego and avoids the harder truth. The disciplined Inquirer asks the question a second time, and often a third, gently but persistently, until the root cause surfaces. That root cause is the only thing worth addressing, because it is the only thing whose resolution will produce lasting change.

Inquiry is also a form of respect. It communicates to the person on the other side of the conversation that you believe they have insight into their own situation, that you are not there to deliver a verdict but to think alongside them, and that your goal is their growth rather than your own sense of having handled a performance issue. Leaders who master the Inquire step become the leaders whose team members actively seek their coaching, because they know those conversations will help them see themselves more clearly.

G — Gain Next Steps

Once the root cause of a behavior has been identified through rigorous Inquiry, the Gain Next Steps step translates that insight into a concrete, collaborative action plan. This is where the conversation shifts from understanding the past to designing the future, and the shift must be made deliberately and together.

Gaining Next Steps is a co-creation process. The leader does not arrive at the conversation with a predetermined improvement plan and announce it. Instead, the leader uses the insights gathered in the Analyze and Inquire phases to invite the person being coached to contribute their own ideas about what needs to change and how. This co-creation is not optional: it is the mechanism that produces ownership rather than compliance. When a person has helped design the path forward, they are significantly more likely to walk it.

The Next Steps that emerge from this phase should meet the SMART criteria: Specific, Measurable, Achievable, Relevant, and Time-bound. Vague commitments like "I'll work on my communication" are not Next Steps. They are aspirations. A real Next Step sounds like: "By next Friday, I will send a brief update to the team after every significant decision, before they have to ask for one." That specificity is what makes accountability possible.

When you apply the Gain Next Steps framework to your own leadership development, the same principles hold. After you have honestly analyzed your behavioral patterns and inquired into their root causes, you need a concrete, time-bound plan for what you are going to do differently. The ALIGN Coaching Model Worksheets in Appendix C are designed to help you build that plan with the specificity it requires.

N — New Commitment

The final step of the ALIGN Coaching Model is both the most important and the most frequently omitted: New Commitment. A great coaching conversation that ends without explicit, mutual commitment to follow-through produces temporary awareness and minimal behavioral change. New Commitment is the step that closes the loop, transforms insight into accountability, and ensures that what was discussed actually becomes what is practiced.

New Commitment means two things. First, it means that the person being coached explicitly commits to the Next Steps that were identified in the previous phase, not just agrees to them in the moment of the conversation, but articulates the commitment clearly and records it in a way that can be reviewed. The ALIGN Coaching Roadmap, which appears in Appendix C, provides the structure for that documentation.

Second, New Commitment means the leader commits to follow-through as well. This includes scheduling specific check-ins to review progress, providing the support or resources the person needs to succeed, and holding the standard that was agreed to without allowing it to quietly fade. The follow-up is what separates a coaching conversation from a coaching relationship, and the coaching relationship is what produces the compounding development that transforms a struggling team member into a high performer.

For you as the leader reading this book, New Commitment also applies to your own development. The reflection questions at the end of every chapter, the FLEX Personality Style Assessment in Appendix A, and the ALIGN Coaching Model Worksheets in Appendix C are only valuable if you make a genuine commitment to using them. Not someday. With a specific date, a specific action, and a specific person in your life who will hold you to it.

ALIGN in Practice: A Complete Picture

Consider Marcus, a team lead at a mid-sized financial services company who has been flagged as a high-potential leader but has struggled to build the trust of his team. He is a natural Controller, decisive and results-oriented, but his team members frequently feel blindsided by his decisions, overlooked in meetings, and reluctant to bring him problems because they expect to receive solutions rather than be heard.

Using the ALIGN Coaching Model, Marcus's manager approaches the situation systematically. She Analyzes the behavioral data: exit interview comments about communication, a team engagement score that has dropped twelve points in eighteen months, and her own observations of how Marcus runs team meetings. She Leverages the Relationship she has built with Marcus through consistent one-on-ones to create enough safety for an honest conversation. Then she Inquires: What does Marcus believe his team most needs from him? What does he think is driving the engagement drop? Why does he tend to make decisions before consulting the team? As the questions deepen, Marcus begins to articulate something he had not fully named before: he moves fast because he is afraid that slowing down will expose gaps in his knowledge that he is not sure how to address.

From that root cause, they Gain Next Steps together. Marcus commits to opening the first fifteen minutes of every team meeting for input before sharing his perspective. He agrees to run his next three major decisions through a brief team consultation process. And he and his manager establish a New Commitment: weekly check-ins for thirty days to review how the new behaviors are landing, with specific metrics for what improvement will look like.

Six months later, Marcus's team engagement score has recovered. His team does not experience him as less decisive. They experience him as someone who values their perspective before acting on his own. He is still a Controller. He is a more complete one.

That is what ALIGN does. It surfaces the real issue, builds the bridge across it, and holds the accountability that makes change stick.

KEY INSIGHT

The ALIGN Coaching Model is not just a tool for coaching your team. It is a framework for understanding yourself with the same precision and honesty you would bring to

---

> developing someone else. The most powerful coaching conversation you will ever have may be the one you have with yourself.

Applying ALIGN to Your Own Leadership

As you move through the rest of this book, you will find the ALIGN Coaching Model woven into every chapter. The FLEX formula steps of Find, Learn, Empathize, and eXpand that form Movement Two are the active expression of the ALIGN Coaching Model applied to personal leadership development. The real-world leadership contexts in Movement Three are where you will practice the ALIGN conversation structure with the people you lead.

Complete the ALIGN Coaching Worksheets in Appendix C. Use them with yourself first, as your own coach. Analyze your leadership behaviors with the same rigor you would bring to analyzing a team member's. Leverage your relationships by being intentional about which connections in your leadership life deserve deeper investment. Inquire honestly into the root causes of the leadership patterns that are not serving you. Gain specific, time-bound Next Steps. And make a New Commitment with a date, an action, and a witness who will hold you to it.

This is not a framework you understand once and then put away. It is a practice that deepens every time you use it. The leaders who apply ALIGN consistently, to their own development and to the development of the people they lead, build a depth of coaching capability and self-knowledge that sets them apart not because they are more talented but because they are more honest with themselves and more committed to the growth of the people around them.

REFLECTION QUESTIONS

1.   Think about a recent leadership conversation that did not produce the change you hoped for. Which step of the ALIGN Coaching Model was missing or incomplete?

2.   Who on your team or in your life would most benefit from an ALIGN-structured conversation right now? What has prevented you from having it?

3.   Apply the Inquire step to yourself: What is one behavioral pattern in your leadership that you have explained away without ever fully examining its root cause?

4.   Write your New Commitment for your own leadership development right now. Make it specific, time-bound, and tell someone who will hold you to it.

This area is for your thoughts:

CHAPTER FOUR

Strengths Are Your Starting Line
Not Your Ceiling

"The most common form of despair is not being who you are."
— Søren Kierkegaard

There is a version of this conversation that I have had hundreds of times in coaching sessions, workshop rooms, and casual hallway conversations with leaders at every level of experience. It usually begins with someone describing a gap: a skill they wish they had, a quality they admire in a colleague, a leadership behavior that does not come naturally to them. And almost always, they describe this gap as the thing standing between the leader they are and the leader they want to be.

There is truth in the desire to grow. There is wisdom in knowing your growth edges. But there is a critical error embedded in the assumption that your weaknesses are your most important leadership project. That assumption has been quietly devastating to leadership development for decades, and it is worth challenging directly before we go any further.

Your strengths are not the starting line for leadership until you acknowledge them fully and choose to leverage them deliberately. Most people dramatically underutilize what they are naturally excellent at, chasing competence in areas of weakness while leaving their areas of genuine mastery at half capacity. This is not development. It is distraction.

Redefining What Strengths Are

A strength is not simply something you do better than the average person. That definition, while useful, is incomplete. A true strength in the context of leadership has three characteristics: it is a natural talent or quality, it produces energy when you engage it rather than depleting you, and it yields results when applied consistently in relevant contexts.

That third element is where leadership strengths become distinctive. A strength that cannot be applied in service of others, that does not translate into better outcomes for teams, projects, communities, or individuals, is more properly a personal skill. Leadership strengths are the ones that, when deployed intentionally, make the people around you more capable, more motivated, or more effective.

Consider the difference between knowing a great deal about a topic and having the strength to communicate complex information in a way that genuinely lands for diverse audiences. Both require knowledge. But the second is a leadership strength because its impact radiates outward. The Thinker who knows everything about a subject but cannot translate that knowledge into accessible insight for their team is carrying an underutilized strength. The Thinker who develops the communication wrapper around their expertise transforms that knowledge into leadership leverage.

The Strengths Inventory: What You Already Have

Every FLEX personality style comes pre-loaded with a set of leadership strengths that are worth naming explicitly and owning without apology. Let's look at what each style naturally brings to the leadership table.

The Feeler's leadership strengths are among the most difficult to quantify but the most viscerally felt. They build trust at a pace that other styles envy, because they are genuinely interested in the people they lead. They create psychological safety without necessarily understanding the academic term for what they are doing. They retain team members because those team members feel seen and valued. They navigate interpersonal conflict with a sophistication that prevents escalation and preserves relationship. In any organization or community, the Feeler is often the invisible architect of the culture, the person whose presence or absence changes everything about how people feel about coming to work.

The Thinker's leadership strengths are in the areas of quality, precision, and strategic depth. They are the leaders you want in the room when the stakes for getting it wrong are high. Their analytical orientation means that the decisions they make are well-considered and defensible. The plans they build are thorough. The standards they set are specific and measurable. They ask questions that improve outcomes and catch errors before they compound. In organizations where accuracy matters, which is to say every organization, the Thinker's strengths are not just useful. They are essential.

The Controller's leadership strengths are in execution, ownership, and pace. They are the leaders who get things done when others are still discussing options. Their directness is a form of respect: they do not waste people's time by being unclear about expectations or feedback. Their high standards, when they are paired with sufficient relational warmth, inspire people to perform at levels they did not previously believe were possible. Organizations in transformation, in crisis, or in competitive environments with thin margins for error particularly depend on the Controller's capacity to hold accountability at every level.

The Entertainer's leadership strengths are in vision, culture, and communication. They are the leaders who can walk into a demoralized team and walk out with a fired-up one, not through manipulation but through genuine belief in what is possible. Their storytelling ability makes complex strategy accessible and memorable. Their enthusiasm is not performance; it is a real orientation toward possibility that is catching. In environments going through change, Entertainers are often the difference between resistance and buy-in, because they can make the case for transformation in terms that feel personally relevant to every person in the room.

Strengths and FLEX Personality Style Together

Here is where the self-awareness work of the previous chapters begins to pay compound dividends. When you know your FLEX personality style and you have honestly identified the strengths that come with that style, you can begin making deliberate choices about where and how to apply them.

This sounds obvious, but it is rarer than it should be. Most people drift into their strengths rather than deploying them strategically. A Feeler might happen to use their relational strengths in some situations but default to a more transactional approach in others, not because the transactional approach is serving them better but because they have not thought consciously about which setting requires what from them.

Strategic strength deployment means you are asking, before every significant leadership moment: What does this situation need? What do I bring that is most relevant to that need? How can I show up in the way that creates the most value here? Those questions are simple. Developing the habit of asking them is not. But that habit is what separates leaders who occasionally do great work from leaders who do great work consistently.

The Starting Line Principle

Your strengths are your starting line. Let me be specific about what that metaphor is doing and not doing. A starting line is not the finish line. Beginning from your strengths does not mean you stay there forever, ignore your growth edges, or never develop new capabilities. That would be a different and much less useful philosophy.

The Starting Line Principle means this: when you begin the race of any leadership challenge from your genuine strengths, you start with momentum. You start with confidence. You start with a natural advantage that you have not had to manufacture. The development work, the growth edge improvement, the new skill acquisition, all of that is built onto a foundation of authentic capability rather than being dragged along behind a desperate attempt to compensate for perceived inadequacy.

I watched the reverse of this principle play out painfully across many years of coaching. Leaders, often in newly elevated roles, would attempt to lead in ways that were entirely misaligned with their natural style because they believed that was what the role required. A natural Feeler who was newly promoted to a senior director role would try to lead like the decisive, data-driven Controller they imagined a senior director was supposed to be. The results were consistently discouraging:

performance below their actual capability, relationships strained by inauthenticity, and confidence steadily eroding.

When those same leaders were coached back to their natural starting line, to their genuine style and their authentic strengths, and then helped to develop their growth edges from that foundation rather than in spite of it, the transformation was often dramatic. Not because they had suddenly become different people. Because they had stopped fighting themselves.

Strengths Are Not Ceilings

The second half of this chapter's title is as important as the first. Strengths are your starting line, not your ceiling. This distinction matters because strength-based development can be misread as a permission slip to never challenge yourself. It is not.

Your dominant FLEX personality style will always be your natural home base. But the most effective leaders I have known across four decades did not simply camp there. They used their home base as the anchor from which they extended their range. A Feeler who developed directness did not stop being a Feeler. They became a Feeler who could deliver difficult feedback without the conversation collapsing under the weight of their discomfort. A Controller who developed patience did not stop being a Controller. They became a Controller whose team learned from the thinking process rather than just scrambling to keep up with the output.

This is what growth edge development looks like when it is done right. It does not erase the strength. It expands the range. It makes the leader more versatile, more adaptive, and more effective in a wider variety of situations. Your ceiling, in other words, is not set by your style. Your ceiling is set by your willingness to grow.

KEY INSIGHT

The most powerful version of you as a leader is not a different style. It is your natural style, fully developed, honestly extended, and deliberately applied. Start from who you are. Grow from there. The ceiling, if there is one, is always higher than you currently believe.

Practical Strength Activation

Let me offer three specific practices for activating your strengths in your current leadership context, regardless of where that context is.

First, name your strengths out loud. Not in an arrogant way, but in the same straightforward way you might tell someone that you are good at driving or cooking. Say it to yourself in the mirror if you need to start there. "I am exceptionally good at building trust quickly." "I have a rare ability to see strategic patterns in complex data." "I can generate more energy around a vision than almost anyone I know." The naming is not performance. It is preparation. You cannot leverage what you have not owned.

Second, look for the situations in your current environment where your strengths are most needed and position yourself there. This is not manipulation. It is good strategic thinking. If you are a natural Thinker and your team is about to make a major decision with insufficient data, speak up. If you are a natural Feeler and a colleague is struggling in a way that others have not noticed, offer your presence. Your strengths are most useful when they meet a genuine need.

Third, use your strengths in service of your growth edge development. If your growth edge is directness and your strength is deep relationship, use the relationships you have built to create the safety that allows you to practice being more direct. If your growth edge is analytical rigor and your strength is enthusiasm, channel that enthusiasm into a genuine curiosity about data that begins to open the analytical door. Strengths are ladders. Use them to reach.

REFLECTION QUESTIONS

1. Name three genuine leadership strengths that come from your FLEX personality style without minimizing or qualifying them. Just name them.

2. In which contexts in your current life are those strengths most needed? Are you showing up in those contexts?

3. Which growth edge could you begin developing using one of your existing strengths as a foundation?

4. What would change in your leadership if you led from your strengths one hundred percent of the time instead of fifty percent?

This area is for your thoughts:

MOVEMENT TWO: DEVELOP - Build the Leader You're Becoming

You now have the foundation: self-knowledge, a personal blueprint, and a clear starting point. Movement Two is where the real building begins. Using the four steps of the FLEX formula, Find, Learn, Empathize, and eXpand, you will develop the specific leadership capabilities that transform awareness into action and intention into impact.

The chapters in DEVELOP are designed to be practiced, not simply read. Each one ends with reflection questions and a specific application challenge. Engage them. The leadership skills in these pages are not theoretical. They are learnable. They are buildable. And they are waiting for you to begin.

CHAPTER FIVE

Find
Knowing Where You Stand

"You can't get to where you're going if you don't know where you are."
— Unknown

There is a story told in leadership circles about a mountain climber who was extraordinarily fit, technically skilled, and deeply motivated to reach the summit. She trained for months, assembled the best equipment, and set out on what she calculated would be a successful three-day ascent. By the end of day one, she was exhausted, disoriented, and camped on the wrong face of the mountain. Her fitness did not fail her. Her equipment did not fail her. Her motivation did not fail her. Her map did. She had started from the wrong coordinates.

Leadership failure follows the same pattern far more often than we acknowledge. The leader is talented. The organization is capable. The goal is worthy. But the diagnosis of the current situation is off, and so every subsequent decision, however well-executed, compounds the misdirection. The most sophisticated strategy in the world is only as useful as the accuracy of the starting point it was built from.

Find is the first step of the FLEX formula, and it is the one that makes everything else work. It is the practice of locating yourself, with honesty and precision, in your current leadership landscape. Where are you? Not where do you want to be. Not where did you used to be. Not where your resume says you are. Where are you actually, right now, as a leader, in the specific context you are currently inhabiting?

What Finding Actually Requires

Finding requires three things that most leaders underinvest in: self-assessment, situational awareness, and the willingness to be honest about what you see.

Self-assessment, in the context of FLEX, begins with the work you have already done: understanding your dominant style, your natural strengths, and your growth edges. But it extends beyond that initial inventory. Effective self-assessment is ongoing and contextual. It asks not just who you are as a leader in general, but how you are showing up in this role, with this team, in this moment.

Situational awareness is the complementary external dimension. It is the ability to read your environment accurately: the culture of the organization or group you are leading in, the dynamics of the team, the pressures and competing priorities that are shaping behavior, the unspoken rules and relationship patterns that are as influential as the formal structures. Leaders who lack situational awareness make decisions that are technically correct and contextually wrong, and they are often the last to understand why.

The willingness to be honest about what you see is the most demanding of the three requirements, because it asks you to resist the very human impulse to interpret your situation in the most favorable light possible. Confirmation bias, the tendency to seek and weigh evidence that confirms what we already believe, is one of leadership's most consequential enemies. Finding requires you to look at the disconfirming evidence with the same attention you give the confirming evidence, and to let the full picture inform your next steps.

The Four Dimensions of Your Current Leadership Position

When I work with leaders on the Find step, I ask them to assess their current situation across four dimensions. Each one tells a different part of the story, and together they create a picture that is comprehensive enough to be genuinely useful.

Dimension 1: Your Influence Currency

How much credibility, trust, and relational capital do you currently hold with the people you are trying to lead? Influence currency is not the same as authority. It is the informal account that you have built, or depleted, through your behavior over time. Every interaction either deposits into that account or withdraws from it: keeping your word deposits, breaking it withdraws; acknowledging others' contributions deposits, taking credit for their work withdraws; showing up prepared deposits, winging it conspicuously withdraws.

Assess your influence currency honestly. With your team, your peers, your direct reports if you have them, your community. Where is the account full? Where is it low? Where has a specific incident created a deficit that you have not yet addressed? Finding this dimension tells you where you can act with authority and where you need to invest before you lead.

Dimension 2: Your Skill-Gap Map

What does your current context require of you that you are not yet fully developed in? This is a different question from what your weaknesses are in general. It is a contextually specific question. A brilliant strategic thinker placed in a role that requires intensive day-to-day people management has a skill gap, not because strategic thinking is not valuable but because the specific demands of the role call for something they have not yet developed.

Map the gap between what your current context requires and what you currently bring. Be specific. Vague skill gaps, things like being more confident or more innovative, are not useful. Specific ones, like developing the ability to run a performance conversation that results in behavioral change without damaging the relationship, are actionable. You can build a development plan around a specific gap. You cannot build one around a vague aspiration.

Dimension 3: Your Energy Audit

Where are you currently spending your leadership energy, and is that where your energy produces the most return? This dimension often reveals uncomfortable truths. Leaders frequently discover that they are spending the majority of their time on tasks that someone else could do, avoiding the conversations that they and only they can have, and deferring the strategic work that would genuinely move their team forward because the administrative work feels more concrete and controllable.

Track your time and your attention for one week without editing. What do you actually do? Where do you actually focus? Then compare that to where you know your highest-value leadership contribution lies. The delta between those two pictures is your energy misalignment, and correcting it is among the highest-return investments you can make.

Dimension 4: Your Relationship Landscape

Who are the key relationships in your current leadership context, and what is the quality and character of each of them? Leadership does not happen in the abstract. It happens between specific people. Your relationship with your direct supervisor shapes your access to resources, support, and opportunity. Your relationship with your peers shapes your ability to collaborate, align, and create lateral influence. Your relationship with those you lead directly shapes every outcome your team produces.

Map your five most important current leadership relationships. For each one, assess: Is this relationship healthy and functional? Is there trust, or is there tension? Is there honest communication, or are things left unsaid that affect the work? What would it take to strengthen this relationship? Finding your relationship landscape tells you where your leadership has natural allies and where it faces headwinds that awareness alone can help you navigate.

Finding in Every FLEX Style

Each FLEX style has a particular relationship with the Find step that is worth naming, because the challenges of honest self-assessment are style-specific.

Feelers can be reluctant to Find when they sense that what they will find is uncomfortable interpersonal territory. They may know, at some level, that a relationship is unhealthy or that a team dynamic is toxic, but the Feeler's aversion to disruption can create a kind of willful blindness. The growth move for the Feeler is to trust that seeing clearly is not the same as acting harshly. You can Find the truth without having to respond to it harshly.

Thinkers can be reluctant to Find when the data is incomplete or when the picture is genuinely ambiguous. The Thinker's preference for precision can lead to an indefinite data-gathering phase that masquerades as diligence but is actually avoidance of a decision that must ultimately be made on imperfect information. The growth move for the Thinker is to establish a sufficient-information threshold and commit to acting once it is reached.

Controllers can be reluctant to Find honestly when what they find does not match their preferred narrative. Controllers often have a strong sense of how things should be and can resist data that challenges that picture. Their speed orientation also works against careful finding, because finding takes time and Controllers are wired to move. The growth move for the Controller is to build the pause into their process deliberately, treating the Find step as mandatory infrastructure rather than optional overhead.

Entertainers can be reluctant to Find when reality is less exciting than vision. The Entertainer's optimism is one of their great gifts, but it can become a liability in the Find step if it causes them to minimize or reframe unfavorable information. The growth move for the Entertainer is to actively seek the perspective of a trusted Thinker or Controller before drawing conclusions, using the contrast as a calibration tool.

The Honest Conversation with Yourself

At its deepest level, Find is a conversation you have with yourself. It is the moment of standing still in the middle of your leadership life, setting down the performance of leadership for just long enough to ask honestly: How am I doing? Not how does it look like I am doing. How am I actually doing?

That question, asked with genuine curiosity rather than judgment, is one of the most powerful leadership moves available to you. It opens the door to information that would otherwise remain invisible because you were too busy performing to see it. It creates the possibility of real growth rather than the appearance of growth.

Make Find a regular practice. Schedule it, literally. Once a month, block sixty minutes for a leadership self-assessment. Use the Appendix C worksheets. Use the reflection questions at the end of each chapter. Use a journal. Use a trusted mentor or peer as a sounding board. The specific mechanism matters less than the commitment to the practice.

Leaders who Find regularly do not get blindsided as often. They course-correct before problems compound. They have conversations that need to be had before silence makes them harder. They do not arrive at a crisis of relevance or impact in their fifties wondering where it all went. They know. And because they know, they navigate.

FIND IN ACTION
(See Appendix D: Find Step – Four Dimensions)

This week, choose one of the four dimensions: influence currency, skill-gap map, energy audit, or relationship landscape. Spend thirty minutes with a notebook assessing yourself in that dimension as honestly as you can. Write down what you see without editing it. Then write down one specific action that information suggests you take. That action is your next leadership step.

REFLECTION QUESTIONS

1.   Which of the four dimensions of your current leadership position is most clear to you right now? Which is most obscured?

2.   Where in your leadership life are you currently operating on assumptions rather than fresh assessment?

3.   What would an honest energy audit of your last week reveal about where your leadership attention is actually going?

4.   Name one relationship in your current leadership landscape that needs more intentional investment. What specifically would that investment look like?

This area is for your thoughts:

CHAPTER SIX

Learn
Growing Through Every Experience

> *"Experience is not the best teacher. Evaluated experience is."*
> — John C. Maxwell

If you have worked for a decade, you might feel confident that you have ten years of leadership experience. But here is a distinction that will reframe that calculation entirely: there is a difference between ten years of experience and one year of experience repeated ten times. The accumulation of time, on its own, does not produce wisdom. The deliberate extraction of insight from time does.

This is the truth behind the Learn step in the FLEX formula. Learning, as a leadership practice, is not passive absorption. It is active excavation. It is the discipline of looking at what happened, understanding why it happened, determining what it means for how you lead going forward, and then actually applying that understanding the next time a similar situation arises. Most people do the first part. Far fewer do all four.

The leaders who grow fastest are not the ones who have the most experiences. They are the ones who extract the most learning from each experience they have. A single difficult conversation, processed with honesty and intention, can teach you more about your communication style than a hundred smooth ones. A project that fails publicly, when examined with intellectual courage, often contains the most precise and relevant insight about your leadership gaps. The question is not what happened to you. The question is what you did with what happened.

The Learning Loop: A Framework for Growth

The Learn step operates through a four-stage loop that, when practiced consistently, transforms every significant leadership experience into growth data.

Stage 1: Experience

This is the event itself. The meeting that went sideways. The decision that produced an unexpected outcome. The conversation that revealed a gap you did not know you had. The project that exceeded every benchmark or collapsed under its own weight. The experience is just the raw material. It is not yet learning.

Stage 2: Reflection

Reflection is where most learning opportunities die. After the experience, the urgent pulls you back into action. The inbox fills. The next meeting begins. The next crisis demands attention. And the experience, with all of its embedded learning, goes unexamined and therefore unretrieved. Reflection requires a deliberate pause, a protected space where you slow down enough to ask: What actually happened there? Not what did I hope would happen, not what should have happened, but what actually happened and why?

Effective reflection is honest without being punishing. It is curious without being defensive. It asks questions rather than rushing to answers. Why did the team respond that way to my approach? What signal did I miss in the early part of that conversation that might have changed how I engaged? What assumption was I operating from that turned out to be inaccurate? What did I do well that I want to replicate?

Stage 3: Insight

Insight is what emerges from sustained, honest reflection. It is the moment when the pattern becomes visible, when the connection between your behavior and the outcome snaps into focus, when you understand something about yourself or your context that you did not understand before. Insight is not always comfortable. In fact, the most valuable insights are often the least comfortable ones.

The quality of your insights depends heavily on the quality of your reflection questions. Shallow questions produce shallow insights. Asking yourself whether something went well produces a yes or no answer that teaches nothing. Asking why it went the way it did, what you specifically did that contributed to the outcome, what you would need to believe differently or do differently to produce a different result, these questions produce insights that are specific enough to be actionable.

Stage 4: Application

Application is where learning becomes leadership. Without it, the first three stages are simply interesting self-examination that produces no behavioral change. Application means you take the insight you have developed and you do something different the next time a similar situation presents itself. Different communication. Different decision process. Different approach to a relationship. Different resource allocation. Whatever the insight has revealed needs to change, application is the act of changing it.

Application is also where you discover whether your insight was accurate. Sometimes the application of an insight produces the expected improvement, confirming your analysis. Sometimes it produces a different result than anticipated, which itself becomes new experience and feeds the loop again. This is why learning is called a loop rather than a line: it is continuous, self-correcting, and cumulative.

What the Best Leaders Learn From

Extraordinary learners extract insight from a wider range of experiences than average learners. Here are the most fertile learning grounds in a leader's landscape, and the specific types of insight each tends to yield.

Failure and adversity are, without question, the most information-rich experiences available to a leader. When things go wrong, every assumption, every habit, every decision gets exposed in high relief. The leader who has never failed at anything significant has also never been given precise data about the boundary of their current capability. Failure, processed with intellectual courage and emotional honesty, is the fastest path to growth available. This does not mean you should seek failure. It means that when it arrives, as it will for every leader who takes real risks, you should mine it relentlessly.

Feedback, both solicited and unsolicited, is a gift that is frequently unwrapped incorrectly. Many leaders hear feedback and immediately sort it into two categories: the feedback that confirms what they believe about themselves (which they accept) and the feedback that challenges what they believe about themselves (which they dismiss as inaccurate, unfair, or politically motivated). That sorting mechanism protects the ego and starves the leader. Effective learning from feedback requires suspending the sorting process long enough to examine the feedback on its own terms: Is there anything useful here? Not is it perfectly delivered, not is it fair in every respect, but is there anything useful here?

Other leaders, especially those whose style, background, and approach differ significantly from your own, are extraordinary learning laboratories. The leader you most disagree with has something to teach you. The leader whose style you find most foreign is modeling a capability you currently lack. Deliberate observation, the practice of watching how effective leaders in your environment handle situations that you also face, is a free, high-quality, always-available development resource that most leaders dramatically underutilize.

The people you lead are among your richest learning sources, and often the most neglected. Your team members know things about your leadership that you cannot know yourself, because they experience it from the receiving end. They know what it feels like when you are in a bad mood and take it out on the quality of your direction. They know when your feedback is actually criticism dressed up as development. They know when you are listening and when you are performing listening. Making it safe for the people you lead to be honest with you about your leadership is one of the most courageous and most productive things you can do.

Learning Across FLEX Personality Styles

Your FLEX personality style shapes not just what you learn but how you learn, and it is worth understanding those tendencies so you can expand your learning range.

Feelers learn most naturally from relationships and conversations. They absorb insight through the felt experience of connection, conflict, reconciliation, and loss. Their challenge is that they sometimes personalize learning in ways that make it emotionally costly rather than simply instructive. A Feeler who processes a leadership failure as a commentary on their worth as a person will avoid the next opportunity for fear of repeating the pain. The growth move is to separate the event from the identity: what happened is not who you are.

Thinkers learn most naturally from analysis and observation. They absorb insight through the careful examination of data, patterns, and principles. Their challenge is that they sometimes prioritize the elegance of their analysis over the messiness of application, and learning that never reaches application is incomplete. The growth move for the Thinker is to set a deadline for reflection and a commitment to application, building the action bridge between insight and behavior.

Controllers learn most naturally from action and outcome. They absorb insight through trial and error, through doing things and seeing what results. Their challenge is that the pace at which they move can outstrip their capacity for reflection, so they repeat mistakes they have not had time to examine. The growth move for the Controller is to build a mandatory reflection window after every significant leadership action, even if it is only ten minutes with a journal.

Entertainers learn most naturally from stories, inspiration, and possibility. They absorb insight through narrative and through connection to larger meaning. Their challenge is that they can fall in love with the story of the learning rather than the discipline of applying it. The growth move for the Entertainer is to translate insight into specific behavioral commitments with accountability structures that hold them to follow-through.

Mentorship and the Accelerated Learning Path

Nothing accelerates leadership learning like a relationship with someone who has navigated the territory you are entering and who is willing to share both their victories and their stumbles with honesty. A mentor is not an authority figure who gives you answers. A mentor is a thinking partner who helps you develop better questions.

I have been both receiver and giver of mentorship throughout my four decades of leadership, and the common thread in every truly transformative mentoring relationship I have witnessed is this: the mentee was willing to be genuinely seen. Not just the polished version of themselves, the impressive career narrative, the carefully curated confidence, but the actual leader, the one with the real doubts and the real mistakes and the real questions. Mentors cannot help you with the performance of leadership. They can only help you with the practice of it.

Seek mentors who are different from you in at least one important way. If you are a Feeler, a mentor who is a strong Thinker or Controller will give you perspectives and challenges that someone with your style simply cannot offer. If you are a Controller, a Feeler mentor may be the person who most reveals the relational dimensions of your impact that you are missing. Difference, in a mentoring relationship, is not a liability. It is the whole point.

And if you are not yet being mentored, begin. Not when you feel ready. Not when you find the perfect candidate. Now. An imperfect mentoring relationship is worth incomparably more than the perfect one you are still waiting to begin.

KEY INSIGHT
(See Appendix E: Learn – The Learning Loop)

Every experience in your leadership life is either teaching you something or confirming something. The difference between growth and stagnation is not the quality of your experiences. It is the quality of your attention to them.

REFLECTION QUESTIONS

1.   Name a significant leadership experience from the past year that you have not fully processed. What insights might be waiting in it?

2.   What type of feedback do you most resist? What might that resistance be protecting you from seeing?

3.   Who in your current context is modeling a leadership capability you want to develop? What specifically can you observe and apply?

4.   If you committed to a fifteen-minute reflection practice after every significant leadership moment, what would you need to change about your current schedule or habits?

This area is for your thoughts:

CHAPTER SEVEN

Empathize
Leading People, Not Just Tasks

---

*"People don't care how much you know until they
know how much you care."*
— Theodore Roosevelt

A few years into my work in the hospitality industry, a senior leader I deeply respected pulled me aside after a team meeting and said something that has stayed with me across all the years since. She said: "You managed that agenda brilliantly. Now tell me: what is actually going on with Marcus?" I did not have an answer. I had noticed that Marcus seemed quieter than usual. I had noticed that his normally sharp contributions to the conversation were subdued. I had filed those observations somewhere in the background and stayed focused on the task.

That leader already knew. She had checked in with Marcus before the meeting and learned that he had received difficult family news the previous evening and was struggling to concentrate. She had adjusted how she engaged him in the meeting, made space for his quietness without drawing attention to it, and ensured he did not leave the room without a private word of support. She had managed the meeting and managed the human being in it simultaneously. I watched her do it and I did not fully see it until she pointed it out.

That moment began my education in the practice of empathy as a leadership skill. Not empathy as a soft virtue, not empathy as an emotional indulgence, but empathy as a precision instrument for understanding the people you are responsible for and responding to them in ways that actually serve them.

What Empathy Is (and Is Not)

Empathy, in the leadership context, is the ability to understand another person's experience, perspective, or emotional state accurately enough to respond to them with genuine relevance. It is not agreement. You can deeply understand why someone feels a certain way and still make a decision that they disagree with. It is not emotional merger, taking on someone else's distress as your own. That is sympathy, and while sympathy is human and valid, it is not the same tool. And it is not performance: the strategic display of care as a technique for managing people. That is manipulation, and it corrodes trust the moment it is detected.

Real empathy in leadership is a perceptive and responsive practice. Perceptive, in that you are consistently gathering information about the inner life of the people around you: their motivations, their concerns, their energy levels, their relationships with each other, their unspoken needs and fears. Responsive, in that you use what you perceive to shape how you lead, what you ask of people, how you communicate, when you press and when you ease off.

Leaders who lead without empathy are not simply less warm than empathetic leaders. They are less effective. They make decisions based on incomplete information because they are missing the human data that empathy would provide. They lose talented people who feel invisible. They miss the early warning signals of team dysfunction because they are not paying attention to the right channels. They generate compliance rather than commitment. Empathy is not optional infrastructure in leadership. It is load-bearing.

The Three Levels of Empathetic Leadership

Developing empathy as a leadership practice is a layered process. I think of it as operating on three levels, each one more demanding and more rewarding than the last.

Level One: Situational Awareness

The first level of empathetic leadership is the ability to read the room. Not literally, though that too, but to develop a practice of continuous environmental scanning that keeps you informed about what is happening with the people around you. Who is engaged and who is checked out? Whose energy has shifted since the last time you worked with them? Who is overloaded and not saying so? Who is being overlooked in a way that is costing your team their contribution?

Situational awareness is built through observation, inquiry, and presence. Observation means watching the nonverbal signals that people send constantly and mostly unconsciously. The meeting participant who has stopped making eye contact. The team member whose normally quick responses have slowed. The colleague whose humor, usually the room's social glue, has gone quiet. Inquiry means asking genuine questions: not "How are you?" as social convention, but "How are you actually?" as a real invitation. Presence means being sufficiently disengaged from your own internal monologue to notice what is happening around you.

Level Two: Perspective-Taking

The second level is deeper: the ability to take another person's perspective with enough accuracy to understand their experience from the inside. This requires setting aside your own frame of reference, however temporarily, and inhabiting another person's view of the same situation.

Perspective-taking is a cognitive skill as much as an emotional one. It asks: If I were in this person's position, with their history, their pressures, their relationships, their context, what would this situation look, feel, and mean to me? That question, when asked honestly, frequently reveals that behavior which seemed unreasonable from the outside makes complete sense from the inside. The team member who pushes back on every new initiative is not resistant to change. They have been promised change before and watched it fail, and their skepticism is rational given their history. The direct report who never volunteers ideas in meetings is not disengaged. They made a suggestion once that was immediately dismissed publicly, and they have been protecting themselves ever since.

Perspective-taking does not require that you agree with the perspective you take. It requires that you understand it. That understanding is what makes it possible to respond in ways that are actually relevant to the person you are trying to lead.

Level Three: Empathetic Response

The third level is the one where empathy produces its most tangible leadership value: the ability to respond to what you have observed and understood in a way that genuinely serves the other person. This is where perception becomes action.

Empathetic response does not always look like comfort or validation. Sometimes the most empathetic response is a clear expectation: I understand that this is hard, and I am also clear that this is what is required. Sometimes it is a challenge: I see what you are capable of better than you see it right now, and this is me refusing to let you settle for less. Sometimes it is simply presence: I am here, I notice, you are not alone in this. The form of the response should follow from the specific need you have accurately perceived.

The leaders who become most trusted in the lives of the people they work with are almost always the ones who have developed this third level of empathetic response. They respond to the real need, not the presented one. They see through the performance of fine to the actuality of struggling and they respond to the struggling. They make people feel, in the fullest sense of that word, understood.

Empathy Across FLEX Personality Styles

Different FLEX personality styles have different starting points and different challenges in the practice of empathy.

Feelers begin at Level Three. Empathetic response is not a skill they need to develop from scratch; it is their natural language. Their challenge is differentiation: learning to tailor their empathetic responses to the specific person in front of them rather than applying their relational warmth uniformly. Not everyone needs the same kind of care, and the Feeler who learns to read which type of empathetic response each individual needs becomes extraordinarily effective.

Thinkers often begin at Level One with genuine skill: their observational acuity is high, and they notice things others miss. Their challenge is in the transition from Level One to Level Two. The analytical framework that makes Thinkers so precise in their reasoning can become a barrier to the non-analytical act of inhabiting another person's emotional experience. The growth move for the Thinker is to practice suspending analysis long enough to feel into a perspective rather than thinking into it.

Controllers often struggle most with Level Two. Their results orientation can make the internal experience of others feel like an inefficient variable rather than a relevant input. When they have a clear goal and a clear plan, the idea of stopping to consider the emotional landscape of their team can feel like a deviation rather than a necessity. The growth move for the Controller is to reframe empathy not as a soft gesture but as a data-gathering exercise that improves the accuracy of their execution strategy.

Entertainers are often naturally strong at the warmth dimension of empathy but can mistake enthusiasm and energy for the kind of attuned attention that genuine empathetic leadership requires. An Entertainer who is working the room may create an experience of warmth without actually seeing the individuals in it. The growth move for the Entertainer is to develop the practice of slowing down, particularly in one-on-one settings, and giving sustained, focused attention rather than high-energy, panoramic engagement.

Empathy in the Hard Moments

The test of empathetic leadership is not how you show up when everything is going well. It is how you show up when someone is struggling, when you have to deliver difficult news, when performance has to be addressed, when a relationship has been damaged and needs to be repaired. These are the moments when most leaders either lean too far into empathy, avoiding necessary directness for fear of causing pain, or too far away from it, delivering hard truths with a bluntness that is technically accurate and humanly corrosive.

The FLEX Leader learns to hold both: the courage to say what is true and the care to say it in a way that the person on the receiving end can actually hear and use. This is one of the highest-order leadership skills, and it is built gradually, through practice, reflection, and a genuine commitment to the belief that people deserve both honesty and humanity at the same time, not alternately, not sequentially, but simultaneously.

When you walk into a difficult conversation with empathy active, you come in curious rather than certain. You come in with a hypothesis about what is happening rather than a verdict. You leave space for the other person's experience to inform your response, and you remain in genuine dialogue rather than simply delivering a prepared message. The outcome of such a conversation is almost always better, for the relationship, for the performance, and for the trust that will determine every future interaction between the two of you.

KEY INSIGHT
(See Appendix F: Empathy – Empathetic Leadership)

The most powerful phrase in the empathetic leader's vocabulary is: Help me understand. Not said as a technique, but as a genuine request. The leader who consistently seeks to understand before they respond will make better decisions, build stronger relationships, and create teams that are capable of far more than any individual within them.

REFLECTION QUESTIONS

1. Who in your current leadership context are you not seeing clearly? What would it take to genuinely understand their experience?

2. Recall a time when you felt truly understood by a leader or mentor. What did they do specifically that created that feeling?

3. What is your most common empathy failure pattern: missing the signal, understanding but not responding, or responding in ways that do not match the actual need?

4. Choose one conversation you need to have this week. Approach it with the question, "Help me understand" as your opening orientation. What are you curious about?

This area is for your thoughts:

eX̲pand
Stretching Beyond Your Comfort Zone

"Life begins at the end of your comfort zone."
— Neale Donald Walsch

There is a region of experience that psychologists call the growth zone. It sits just beyond the edge of what you currently do comfortably. Not so far beyond it that the challenge becomes paralyzing, but far enough beyond it that your current capabilities are not quite sufficient and you have to reach, stretch, and build new capacity to succeed. The growth zone is where leadership development actually happens, and it is a place most people visit only accidentally, when circumstances force them there.

The eXpand step in the FLEX formula is about changing that dynamic. It is about choosing to enter the growth zone deliberately, strategically, and regularly, rather than waiting for life to push you there involuntarily. It is the recognition that the version of you that exists on the far side of a genuine challenge is always more capable than the version of you that avoided it, and that every deliberate stretch builds the range you will need for the leadership that is still ahead of you.

After four decades of leading and watching leaders develop, I can tell you with confidence: the leaders who most consistently expand their range are the ones who most consistently create extraordinary outcomes. Not because they take reckless risks or because they are naturally more courageous than others, but because they have built a practice of deliberate expansion that compounds over time into a breadth of capability that more cautious leaders simply cannot match.

The Anatomy of Expansion

Expansion is not a single act. It is a sequence of choices, each one building on the last. Understanding the anatomy of that sequence makes expansion more accessible, less mysterious, and significantly more repeatable.

The Recognition Point

Every expansion begins with the recognition that the current approach is insufficient. Something in your environment is signaling that what you have been doing is not producing what is needed, or that an opportunity exists that your current capability cannot capture. The recognition point is often uncomfortable: it is the moment you feel the gap between where you are and where you want or need to be.

Many leaders turn away at the recognition point. The gap feels too large, the self-concept too threatened, the risk of visible failure too high. Turning away is always a choice, and it always has consequences: the growth that does not happen, the capability that does not develop, the leadership that does not reach its potential. The eXpand step begins with the decision to turn toward the recognition point rather than away from it.

The Deliberate Stretch

Once you have recognized the growth opportunity, the deliberate stretch is the specific action you take to engage it. This is not generic challenge-seeking. It is targeted: identifying the specific capability, behavior, or perspective that your current context is calling for and taking a specific action to begin developing it.

Deliberate stretches can take many forms. Taking on a leadership role or responsibility that exceeds your current comfort level. Having a conversation you have been avoiding because it requires a directness or vulnerability you have not practiced. Volunteering for a project in an area where you have limited expertise. Asking for feedback from someone whose perspective is likely to be challenging. Presenting to an audience that intimidates you. The specific stretch matters less than the deliberateness of it: you are not stumbling into difficulty. You are choosing to engage growth.

The Discomfort Period

Here is something worth knowing in advance: expansion is uncomfortable during the process. This is not a design flaw. It is evidence that growth is occurring. Your brain, confronted with a demand that exceeds your current wiring, works to build new pathways. That process is neurologically and psychologically demanding, and it produces a characteristic experience of uncertainty, awkwardness, and occasional discouragement.

The discomfort period is the point at which most growth attempts fail, not because the challenge was too great but because the discomfort was misinterpreted as evidence that the challenge was wrong. It was not. The discomfort is temporary. The capability it is building is permanent. Knowing this in advance does not eliminate the discomfort, but it transforms its meaning from "I am failing" to "I am growing," and that distinction makes an enormous difference to whether you persist.

The Integration Phase

Expansion has an integration phase, a period after the acute stretch during which what you have been developing begins to feel more natural and more yours. This is when the growth becomes permanent: when the skill moves from conscious effort to practiced capability, when the new behavior becomes part of your default leadership range rather than something you have to consciously deploy.

Integration does not happen automatically. It requires continued practice in lower-stakes settings to consolidate the gains made in higher-stakes ones. The leader who delivered a challenging presentation to an executive team for the first time, and survived, will benefit enormously from delivering five more presentations to progressively easier audiences in the weeks that follow. The capability is built in the stretch. It is consolidated in the repetition.

What Genuine Expansion Looks Like by FLEX Personality Style

Each FLEX personality style has characteristic expansion challenges that are worth naming because they are predictable. Knowing yours in advance allows you to approach them with preparation rather than surprise.

For Feelers, expansion often means developing the capacity for direct, clear communication in situations where the relational cost feels high. The Feeler who learns to say, clearly and kindly, "This performance is not meeting the standard, and here is what needs to change" has expanded their range in one of the most practically important ways. They have not stopped being a Feeler. They have become a Feeler who can hold people accountable with warmth and precision simultaneously.

For Thinkers, expansion often means developing comfort with action under conditions of imperfect information, and with communication styles that are more fluid and relational than their natural precision prefers. The Thinker who learns to give a spontaneous, emotionally resonant team briefing without a prepared script has expanded their range in a way that dramatically increases their organizational influence.

For Controllers, expansion often means developing patience with process and people. The Controller who learns to slow down enough to bring their team along, to explain their reasoning rather than simply issuing direction, to tolerate the pace of collaborative development rather than always defaulting to unilateral decision-making, has expanded their range in a way that makes their organizations significantly more durable.

For Entertainers, expansion often means developing follow-through systems and detail orientation. The Entertainer who learns to hold themselves to the specifics of commitments they have made, who builds the structural habits that translate vision into reliable execution, who shows up to the unsexy administrative dimensions of leadership with the same energy they bring to the inspirational ones, has expanded their range in a way that makes their charisma sustainable rather than episodic.

Strategic Courage

I want to introduce a concept that I have found invaluable across four decades of both practicing and coaching leadership: **strategic courage**. It is distinct from impulsive risk-taking, which is not courage but recklessness. And it is distinct from performing courage while privately staying safe, which is not courage at all.

Strategic courage is the deliberate decision to take a meaningful risk in service of a worthy goal, with honest awareness of the consequences and genuine acceptance of the possibility that it might not work. It is courage that has done its homework. It is courage that is informed by a clear understanding of what is at stake, what the realistic range of outcomes is, and what you are prepared to learn from either outcome.

Strategic courage shows up in leadership constantly, in ways that do not always look dramatic from the outside. The courage to give someone honest feedback that might strain the relationship but could change their trajectory. The courage to advocate for an idea that has merit but faces organizational resistance. The courage to admit, publicly, that you were wrong about something. The courage to take on a role or a challenge that is genuinely uncertain, because the growth it offers is genuinely necessary.

Building a practice of strategic courage is one of the highest-value commitments you can make as a leader. It is what prevents the slow, comfortable, incremental narrowing that happens to leaders who stop stretching. And it is what keeps your leadership alive, relevant, and growing at every stage of the journey.

THE EXPANSION COMMITMENT
(See Appendix G: eXpand – Expansion Growth Zone)

This month, identify one specific expansion challenge: one conversation, one role, one responsibility, one skill that is just beyond your current comfortable range. Commit to engaging it before the month ends. Write it down. Tell

---

someone who will hold you to it. The act of naming it and committing it to it is the first step of the stretch.

REFLECTION QUESTIONS

1.   What is the most significant expansion your leadership has undergone in the past two years? What made it possible?

2.   What growth opportunity are you currently aware of but have been choosing not to engage? What is the real reason you have not engaged it?

3.   What would you attempt in your leadership if you knew the discomfort period was temporary and the growth was permanent?

4.   Name one person in your life who could serve as an accountability partner for your expansion commitment. Have you told them?

This area is for your thoughts:

CHAPTER NINE

Leading Across Styles
When Your FLEX Meets Other FLEX Types

> *"In diversity there is beauty and there is strength."*
> — Maya Angelou

Everything in the first eight chapters has been primarily about you: your style, your ALIGN blueprint, your Find, Learn, Empathize, and eXpand journey. That self-focus was not narcissism. It was necessary groundwork. You cannot lead others effectively if you do not understand yourself accurately. But leadership, by definition, happens between people, and the most important application of everything you have learned is what happens when your FLEX personality style meets someone else's.

Here is a truth that will save you enormous frustration if you carry it into every leadership relationship you have: when someone responds to you in a way that seems difficult, unreasonable, disorganized, slow, cold, overwhelming, or wrong, they are almost never doing it at you. They are almost always doing it from their style. And your frustration with them is almost always your style interpreting their style through your own lens and finding it insufficient. That friction is not evidence of incompatibility. It is evidence of different wiring. And different wiring, understood and navigated well, is an organizational superpower.

The FLEX Interaction Matrix

Let's examine the most common cross-style dynamics in leadership relationships, identifying both the natural tension and the path through it.

Feeler + Controller

This is one of the most common tension pairs in organizational life. The Feeler's relationship-first approach can feel to the Controller like inefficiency, like an obstacle to getting things done. The Controller's results-first approach can feel to the Feeler like a lack of care, like people are being treated as instruments rather than human beings. Both interpretations are understandable and both are incomplete.

The Feeler brings to this relationship something the Controller needs desperately: the relational intelligence that makes a Controller's high-standard environment survivable for the team. Without the Feeler's warmth, a Controller-led environment can produce excellent short-term results and devastating long-term turnover. The Controller brings something the Feeler equally needs: the directness that turns good intentions into measurable outcomes, the willingness to make the call when consensus would take too long, the clarity of expectation that makes Feeler-led environments more accountable. Together, they create something neither could alone.

If you are a Feeler working with or for a Controller: stop interpreting their directness as an attack. Deliver your ideas with the outcome-focused language they respond to. "I think building this relationship will directly improve our retention numbers" will land better than "I feel like we need to be warmer with the team." Speak their language. If you are a Controller working with or for a Feeler: slow down long enough to acknowledge the people dimension before driving to the result. Three extra minutes of genuine check-in before a meeting will save you thirty minutes of managing resistance after it.

Thinker + Entertainer

This is another high-friction pairing with extraordinary potential. The Thinker finds the Entertainer's enthusiasm exhausting and their follow-through unreliable. The Entertainer finds the Thinker's caution suffocating and their pace frustrating. Both are seeing real things. Neither is seeing the full picture.

The Thinker brings analytical rigor to the Entertainer's vision, transforming exciting ideas into executable plans by identifying what has been overlooked, what the risks are, and what the gap between aspiration and reality looks like. Without the Thinker, Entertainer-led initiatives often generate excitement that dissipates when the execution plan proves to be shallower than the vision. The Entertainer brings energy and narrative to the Thinker's precision, making their carefully constructed analysis accessible, compelling, and actionable for audiences who would otherwise never engage with it. Without the Entertainer, Thinker-led initiatives often produce excellent work that nobody uses because nobody got excited enough about it to implement it.

If you are a Thinker working with an Entertainer: lead with the possibility before you inventory the problems. Your analytical flags are valuable, but delivered first, they shut down the generative conversation the Entertainer needs to have. If you are an Entertainer working with a Thinker: do not interpret their questions as resistance. They are the quality control your vision needs. Give them the time and data they are asking for. Their thoroughness is the thing that will make your idea work.

Feeler + Thinker

Feelers and Thinkers often struggle to find common communication ground. The Feeler communicates through connection and context, the Thinker through data and logic, and conversations between them can feel like they are happening in different languages.

The Feeler can help the Thinker understand the human impact of analytically-derived decisions in ways that make those decisions more sustainable. People are not variables, and even the most elegant analytical framework will encounter friction when it meets actual human behavior; the Feeler can serve as the translator. The Thinker can help the Feeler build structures and systems around their relational strengths that produce consistency rather than inspired but episodic performance. Their partnership, when it works, produces decisions that are both rigorously designed and humanely implemented.

Controller + Entertainer

The Controller-Entertainer pair can generate extraordinary momentum when aligned and significant chaos when not. The Controller wants to execute; the Entertainer wants to inspire. When the inspiration and the execution point in the same direction, they are nearly unstoppable together. When they diverge, the Controller gets frustrated with what feels like distraction and the Entertainer feels constrained by what feels like rigid control.

The key to this partnership is sequencing: let the Entertainer create the vision and the buy-in, then let the Controller build the execution infrastructure and hold the accountability. Each does what they do best. Neither overrides the other. The Controller's respect for the Entertainer's relational reach grows when they see it translating into results. The Entertainer's respect for the Controller's discipline grows when they see it turning their inspiration into reality.

Leading People Who Are Different from You

The most practically important application of cross-style awareness is not in your peer relationships. It is in how you lead people whose style is different from yours. Your team is almost certainly not a room full of people who are wired like you. And the way you naturally prefer to be led is not the way everyone on your team needs to be led.

This is one of the most common sources of leadership failure I have observed: leaders who lead everyone the way they themselves want to be led. The Controller who delivers feedback bluntly because that is what they would want, to a team member who needs more context and care to receive feedback effectively. The Feeler who softens difficult messages to the point of ambiguity because they want to protect people from discomfort, to a team member who desperately needs clarity and is frustrated by the hedging. The Thinker who communicates in dense detail because that is their preference, to a team member who needs the big picture before the details or they lose the thread entirely.

Adapting your leadership approach to the style of the person you are leading is not the sacrifice of your authenticity. It is the highest expression of it. It means you care enough about the person in front of you to meet them where they are rather than requiring them to always come to you.

The Versatility Advantage

Leaders who develop genuine versatility across the FLEX personality range, who can flex their natural style to meet the needs of different people, different situations, and different challenges, are among the most organizationally valuable leaders available. They do not replace their dominant style. They extend their range.

Versatility is built gradually. It begins with awareness, which you now have. It develops through practice: deliberately choosing a less natural approach in situations where your natural one is not serving the moment. A Controller who practices patience with a slow-processing Feeler team member, not grinding their teeth and tolerating it but genuinely slowing down and creating space. A Feeler who practices directness with a Controller peer who needs to hear the bottom line first and the context second. An Entertainer who practices structured follow-through with a Thinker partner who needs to see the detail to trust the vision.

Each of these practices is uncomfortable at first, which is why they qualify as eXpand challenges. They each require you to operate in a range that is not your natural center. But the leaders who build this versatility over time become, simply, more effective with more people in more situations. That is not a minor advantage. In a complex, diverse, constantly changing world, it may be the defining leadership advantage.

KEY INSIGHT

The goal of cross-style leadership is not to become all four FLEX personality styles equally. It is to develop enough fluency in the other styles to lead the people who operate from them more effectively. Your home base stays yours. Your range expands. Your impact multiplies.

REFLECTION QUESTIONS

1.   Which FLEX personality style do you find most challenging to work with? What specifically creates the friction?

2.   Think of a current relationship with someone whose style is very different from yours. What is the complementary gift they bring that you tend to overlook in the friction of the difference?

3.   Name one adjustment in your communication or leadership approach that would better serve someone on your team whose style differs from yours.

4.   Where in your current leadership context are you leading everyone the same way? What would individualized leadership look like there?

This area is for your thoughts:

MOVEMENT THREE: DEPLOY - Make Your Mark

Everything you have discovered and developed exists in service of this: the leadership you will practice in the real contexts of your real life, with real people, in real time. Movement Three is about deployment, about taking everything this book has built in you and releasing it into the world where it can do the work it was always meant to do.

This movement will take you through the specific contexts where your leadership operates, through the hard moments when leadership asks more than you feel capable of giving, and all the way to the question of legacy: not what leadership is, but what yours will mean.

You are ready for this. You have been ready longer than you knew.

CHAPTER TEN

Leading in Real Life
School, Work, Home, Community

"Leadership is not a role. It is a responsibility you choose, in every room you enter."
— Shaine Hobdy, Author

The frameworks, the self-knowledge, the cross-style fluency, all of it only matters insofar as it touches the actual contexts where you live and lead. The greatest leadership development program ever designed produces nothing if it does not translate into the classroom, the conference room, the kitchen table, and the community meeting. This chapter is about that translation.

One of the most liberating insights I can offer you at this point in the book is this: you do not lead differently in different contexts because you are a different person. You lead the same essential person, with the same FLEX personality style, the same ALIGN Coaching Model blueprint, the same strengths and growth edges, in contexts that have different norms, different stakes, different relationships, and different success criteria. Understanding those contextual differences allows you to show up with the right expression of your leadership for each setting, without losing the consistent core of who you are.

Leading in School

If you are a student, you are already leading. You may not be calling it that, and your school may not be recognizing it as that, but the influence you have on the people around you, for better or worse, is real and consequential.

Academic settings offer one of the most information-rich leadership laboratories available, precisely because the stakes are high enough to demand real engagement but low enough to allow recovery from mistakes. The student who organizes a group project and learns how to coordinate people with different work styles is learning stakeholder management. The student who speaks up in class when everyone else is silent is practicing public advocacy. The student who mentors a struggling classmate is developing coaching capability. None of these require a student leadership title. All of them are real leadership.

The specific leadership challenge of school settings is the social complexity of peer leadership. Leading peers, people who see themselves as your equals and have not formally consented to your leadership, requires the highest order of informal leadership skills. You cannot rely on authority. You can only rely on credibility, on the quality of your ideas, the consistency of your follow-through, the genuineness of your care, and the competence of your contribution. These are the leadership muscles that will serve you most powerfully for the rest of your life, and school is where you build them.

If you hold a formal student leadership role, whether that is a student government position, a team captaincy, a club leadership role, or any other, resist the temptation to use the title as your primary leadership tool. The most effective student leaders I have observed treat their title as a responsibility, not an authority. They use their position to open doors for others, to advocate for the needs of the broader group, to create experiences that would not exist without their initiative. Their followers do not follow them because they have to. They follow because they want to.

Leading in the Workplace

The workplace is where most people first encounter leadership as a structured, evaluated practice. And it is where most people first discover the gap between the leader they imagined they would be and the leader they currently are. That gap is not a problem. It is the curriculum.

Workplace leadership operates across a spectrum of formality. At the most informal end, you are leading through influence, expertise, and relationship even if your business card does not say manager. At the most formal end, you are managing direct reports with official accountability for their performance and development. In between is a vast range of project leadership, cross-functional collaboration, client relationship management, and stakeholder navigation that constitutes the bulk of what most working leaders actually do.

Across all of those contexts, the principles from the first nine chapters apply directly. Your FLEX personality style shapes how you communicate, how you make decisions, and how you build relationships at work. Your ALIGN Coaching Model blueprint provides the structure for your ongoing development. The FLEX formula gives you the four-step process for continuously improving your leadership effectiveness in the specific challenges your workplace presents.

One specific workplace leadership challenge worth naming directly: managing up. Most leadership development focuses on leading the people below you in the organizational hierarchy, but some of the most consequential leadership in any organization happens upward, when someone exercises genuine influence on the people who have authority over them. Managing up effectively, helping your leaders make better decisions, advocating for your team and your ideas with credibility and appropriate persistence, building a genuine relationship of trust and mutual respect with people in positions of authority, is a leadership skill that is rarely taught and almost always developed through hard experience. The FLEX Leadership System and the ALIGN Coaching Model frameworks are as applicable to these upward relationships as they are to every other leadership context.

Leading at Home

I want to name this context because it is often the one people forget to include when they think about their leadership, and it is frequently the most important one. The leadership you practice in your household, whether you are a parent, a partner, a sibling, a caregiver, or simply the person who the people you live with tend to look to, is real leadership. It is also the leadership with the longest time horizon and the deepest stakes.

The dynamics of home leadership are unique in one crucial respect: the relationships are not optional. In a workplace, a difficult leadership relationship can, ultimately, be exited. The people we lead at home, the children we are raising, the partners we are building lives with, the aging parents we are caring for, are not people we can choose to stop leading if it gets hard. That permanence demands a level of leadership commitment and quality that exceeds even the most demanding professional context.

Feelers often find home leadership their most natural context, though they may struggle with the boundary-setting and accountability dimensions that family life requires. Controllers can be extraordinary in creating structure and safety at home but may need to consciously cultivate warmth and patience in the family context. Thinkers may excel in the analytical dimensions of family decision-making but benefit from deliberate effort to create emotional connection. Entertainers bring genuine joy and energy to family culture but need structural support to maintain the consistency that family relationships require.

One of the most powerful things I have learned about home leadership is this: the children and young people in your life are watching your leadership almost continuously. Not your leadership at work. Your leadership at home. How you handle conflict. How you respond to disappointment. Whether your words and your behavior are aligned. Whether you take responsibility when you make mistakes or whether you deflect and explain. The leadership model you embody at home is the most direct and lasting contribution you will ever make to the next generation of leaders. Take it seriously.

Leading in Community

Community leadership is the arena where purpose often meets its fullest expression. Whether you are involved in a faith community, a neighborhood association, a nonprofit, a youth program, or any other form of civic or social organization, community leadership allows you to apply your gifts in service of something that is larger than your career and outlasts any single role you occupy.

Community leadership is also where informal leadership skills, the ones we talked about at the beginning of this book, matter most. Community organizations rarely have the formal authority structures of workplaces. Volunteers are not obligated in the way employees are. Board members are peers, not subordinates. Influence in community settings must be earned continuously, renewed regularly, and exercised with a generosity of spirit that keeps people willing to follow even when it is difficult.

If you are not currently involved in community leadership of any kind, I encourage you to consider it. Not as a burden, but as an opportunity. The leadership muscles you build in community service are unlike the ones you build in any other context, and the perspective you gain from serving people whose lives are very different from your own is irreplaceable. Some of the wisest, most effective organizational leaders I have ever known spent their most formative leadership years not in corporate training programs but in community organizations where they had to learn, through necessity, how to lead without authority, inspire without compensation, and build sustainable institutions out of commitment rather than compliance.

The Unified Leader

Here is an aspiration worth carrying: the unified leader is someone whose leadership does not fragment across contexts. Their values are the same at work and at home. Their commitment to growth does not disappear when they leave a formal development setting. Their empathy is not a workplace skill they put on with their professional clothes; it is a practice they bring to every room they enter.

Becoming a unified leader is not about achieving perfection in every context simultaneously. It is about developing the consistent character that is recognizable across all of your contexts, the people in your life being able to see the same essential person in all of the roles you inhabit. That consistency is the deepest form of authenticity, and it is one of the rarest and most admirable qualities in any leader at any level.

Your ALIGN Coaching Model practice is designed to support that kind of unified development. When you are Analyzing your own behaviors, the data you gather is relevant at work and at home. When you are Leveraging Relationships, the trust you build crosses every boundary in your life. When you Inquire with genuine curiosity, it serves your community role and your parenting role and your peer relationships equally. The investment you make in yourself as a leader through the ALIGN model is never context-specific. It is a compound return across every dimension of your life.

REFLECTION QUESTIONS

1.   In which of the four contexts (school, work, home, community) is your leadership currently strongest? What makes it work there?

2.   In which context is your leadership most inconsistent or underdeveloped? What is the specific challenge?

3.   Name one person in your household or family whose development you influence directly. How intentional are you about that influence?

4.   What community involvement, if you were fully engaged with it, would allow your leadership strengths to serve something beyond your immediate career or family?

This area is for your thoughts:

CHAPTER ELEVEN

When Leadership Gets Hard
Failure, Doubt, and Resilience

"It is not the critic who counts, not the man who points out how the strong man stumbles. The credit belongs to the man who is actually in the arena."
— Theodore Roosevelt

I want to write this chapter with particular care, because what I have to say in it is not comfortable, and the temptation when writing about leadership is always to keep things inspiring and leave the hard parts vague. That temptation, indulged, produces the kind of leadership content that feels good to read and fails to prepare you for anything real. Real leadership is hard. Sometimes it is very hard. And the leaders who endure and grow through the hard parts are not exceptional human beings. They are ordinary people who made a specific set of choices about how to relate to difficulty.

Across forty years of leading and watching leaders, I have collected a library of leadership failures. Not other people's failures, observed from a safe distance, but my own, intimate and instructive. Decisions that did not produce what I anticipated. Relationships I failed to protect or repair. Teams I let down by not seeing something clearly enough. Moments where I was not the leader the situation required and I knew it and could not reach the version of myself that would have made it different. Those failures are not the parts of my story I am most proud of. But they are, without exception, the parts that taught me the most.

Failure as Curriculum

The leadership culture we have inherited treats failure as primarily a source of shame. It is something to be explained away, minimized in interviews, framed as a learning on resumes, and generally hidden from public view as quickly and thoroughly as possible. That relationship with failure is not only psychologically damaging. It is strategically disastrous.

Failure is data. Specific, high-fidelity data about the precise boundary of your current capability. It tells you exactly where your assumptions were wrong, where your skills were insufficient, where your judgment was off, and where you needed support you did not have or did not ask for. No other information source is this honest, this specific, or this personally calibrated. A hundred hours of leadership development programming will not give you the diagnostic precision of one well-processed failure.

Processing failure well means engaging it with intellectual courage rather than retreating from it with emotional self-protection. It means asking: What happened, specifically? What role did my decisions play in the outcome? What was in my control that I did not use well? What was outside my control that I need to factor into my next attempt? What does this tell me about a specific gap in my capability that I can now intentionally develop? These questions are not comfortable. They are productive. And the answers they produce are the curriculum for the next level of your leadership.

The leaders I have watched recover most impressively from failure are almost always the ones who faced it most directly. They did not spend weeks or months in denial or self-pity. They named what happened, they examined it, they identified what they needed to do differently, and they began doing it. The recovery was not always fast, but it was always forward.

The Specific Shape of Doubt

Doubt is the companion that follows every leader who is attempting anything worth doing. It is not a signal that you are wrong for the role, insufficient for the challenge, or destined for failure. It is a signal that what you are doing matters enough to be scary. Doubt and significance travel together.

The specific shape of doubt varies by FLEX personality style. Feelers tend to doubt their worth through the lens of relationship: Am I liked enough? Have I disappointed the people who matter to me? Am I capable of managing the interpersonal complexity this leadership requires? Thinkers tend to doubt through the lens of competence: Have I thought through this thoroughly enough? Is my analysis correct? Am I missing something critical that I will discover too late? Controllers tend to doubt through the lens of performance: Am I producing enough? Am I moving fast enough? Are my results good enough to justify the position I hold? Entertainers tend to doubt through the lens of impact: Does anyone actually care what I am doing? Is the vision I am promoting real or is it just excitement? Will this actually make a difference?

Each of these doubt patterns has a specific antidote. Feeler doubt responds to evidence of real connection: a specific conversation, a genuine expression of trust, a relationship that has survived a difficult passage. Thinker doubt responds to evidence of competence: a completed analysis reviewed by a trusted peer, a decision that produced the predicted outcome, a problem solved through the application of rigorous thinking. Controller doubt responds to evidence of results: a milestone reached, a metric moved, an obstacle cleared. Entertainer doubt responds to evidence of impact: a person who tells them specifically what changed because of their leadership, a community that is measurably different from how it was.

Name your doubt pattern. Know its shape. Know what evidence helps. And then, when doubt arrives, which it will, treat it as information rather than verdict. It is telling you that you care, that the stakes are real, and that you are not sleepwalking through your leadership. Those are all good signs.

Imposter Syndrome: The Leader's Persistent Shadow

Imposter syndrome, the persistent fear that you are not as qualified as people believe and that you will eventually be found out, is extraordinarily common among high-performing leaders. Research suggests that the phenomenon is essentially universal among ambitious people, meaning that the leaders most plagued by the feeling that they do not belong in the room are often the ones who most deserve to be there.

Understanding imposter syndrome does not make it disappear. But it does reframe it usefully. If you are experiencing imposter syndrome, it is almost certainly evidence of at least three positive realities: you are in a context that is stretching you, which is exactly where growth happens; you have enough self-awareness to know the gap between where you are and where you want to be; and you care enough about doing well that the fear of doing poorly is real.

The practical response to imposter syndrome is not the suppression of the feeling, which does not work and is exhausting to attempt. It is the development of a practice that separates the feeling from the fact. The feeling says: I do not belong here and I am about to be exposed. The fact often says: I have been effective in this role, I have evidence of my competence, the people who put me in this position saw something real, and the work I have done has had genuine impact. Keep both in view. Let the fact inform your behavior even when the feeling is loud.

Building Leadership Resilience

Resilience is not the absence of difficulty. It is the capacity to engage difficulty without being permanently diminished by it. It is the ability to be knocked down, to experience the full weight of the landing, and then to make a choice, not to pretend it did not hurt, not to instantly perform recovery, but to genuinely and thoughtfully get back up.

Building leadership resilience is an ongoing practice rather than a fixed capacity, and it rests on several foundations that can be intentionally developed.

The first foundation is a clear and stable sense of identity. Leaders who know who they are at the level of values and character are significantly more resilient than leaders who have tied their identity to their title, their performance metrics, or others' approval. When the title disappears, when the metrics dip, when the approval is withdrawn, the leader whose identity was tied to those things has very little left to stand on. The leader whose identity is built on values, on the knowledge of who they are and what they stand for, has something no external circumstance can take away.

The second foundation is an honest support network. Resilience is not a solo project. The leaders who recover most effectively from difficulty are almost always the ones who have people in their lives who know them truly, who can bear witness to the difficulty without trying to solve it away, and who can speak honest perspective when the leader's own perspective has become too narrow to be useful. Building those relationships is not a luxury. It is a strategic necessity.

The third foundation is a practice of self-care that you are willing to maintain under pressure. This may be the most commonly neglected foundation in leadership resilience, because leaders often treat self-care as a reward for performing well rather than a requirement for performing at all. The leader who stops sleeping, stops exercising, stops connecting with people they love, and stops doing the things that genuinely restore them, under the belief that the organization's needs take priority, will eventually have nothing left to give the organization. Your capacity to lead is not separate from your wellbeing. It is an expression of it.

The fourth foundation is a long-term perspective. Most of what feels catastrophic in the short term looks significantly different from a longer view. The project that failed becomes the insight that informed the next ten. The relationship that fractured becomes the lesson in the communication pattern you no longer repeat. The role you did not get becomes the period of development that made you ready for a better one. Resilience is built partly in the moment, when you choose to get up rather than stay down, and partly in the narrative, when you learn to see the arc of your leadership life as coherent, developmental, and moving toward something.

KEY INSIGHT
The question for every difficult leadership moment is not: Why is this happening to me? The question is: What is this developing in me? That single reframe does not make difficulty comfortable. It makes it purposeful. And purpose is what resilience runs on.

When to Ask for Help

No chapter on resilience would be complete without addressing one of the most consistent leadership failure patterns I have witnessed: the unwillingness to ask for help. Leaders, particularly those with strong Controller or Thinker tendencies, can develop an identity built around self-sufficiency that becomes a prison rather than a strength.

Asking for help is not evidence of insufficiency. It is evidence of wisdom. The leader who knows what they do not know, who has the clarity to see where their current capacity is insufficient for the current challenge, and who has the humility to reach for the support that will make the difference, is a more capable leader than the one who white-knuckles through challenges they could navigate more effectively with a wider support network.

Ask for help early, when it is a choice, rather than late, when it is a crisis. Ask specifically rather than generally: not "I need help" but "I need someone with experience in X to think through this decision with me." And build the relationships with mentors, peers, coaches, and trusted advisors now, before you need them desperately, so that when difficult moments arrive, the support network is already in place.

> **REFLECTION QUESTIONS**
>
> 1.   What is your most consistent pattern when leadership gets hard? Do you push through, withdraw, seek support, or something else?
>
> 2.   Name a failure from your leadership history that you have not fully processed. What specific insight might still be waiting in it?
>
> 3.   What does your doubt sound like? What specific evidence most effectively quiets it?
>
> 4.   What self-care practices are you consistently sacrificing in the name of productivity? What would change if you treated those practices as non-negotiable?

This area is for your thoughts:

CHAPTER TWELVE

Your Leadership Legacy Starts Now
The Leader You're Already Becoming

"The greatest use of a life is to spend it for something that will outlast it."
— William James

We are approaching the end of this book and the beginning of something much larger. I want to start this final chapter by asking you a question that most leadership books save for motivational speeches and never actually answer: What are you building, beyond yourself?

Legacy is a word that can feel remote, reserved for people who have already accomplished significant things and are now considering how those accomplishments will be remembered. But legacy is not a reward that comes after a long career. It is a practice that begins the moment you choose to lead with intention. Every interaction you have with someone in your sphere of influence is either building your legacy or eroding it. Every decision you make under pressure either reinforces or undermines the leader you are becoming. Legacy is not what happens after you are gone. It is what is already happening while you are here.

Defining What Matters

The first work of legacy is the work of definition. Not what others have decided should matter to a leader, not what the culture you inhabit says success looks like, but what you, knowing your FLEX personality style, your values, your ALIGN Coaching Model blueprint, and the people and causes you most care about, determine to be the central purpose of your leadership.

Purpose-driven leadership is not a concept reserved for nonprofit founders or social entrepreneurs. It is available to every leader in every context. The customer service manager who is driven by the conviction that every person deserves to be treated with dignity and who builds that conviction into every system, every policy, and every team expectation they create is leading with as much purpose as any CEO with a world-changing mission statement. The teacher who decides that every student in their class will leave with at least one experience of genuine intellectual excitement is leading a legacy as significant as any elected official. Purpose is not determined by the scale of your platform. It is determined by the clarity of your commitment.

Take some time, before the end of this chapter, to write a legacy statement. Not a mission statement full of impressive words, but a plain-language articulation of what you want to have contributed by the end of your leadership journey. What capabilities do you want to have built in the people you led? What conditions do you want to have created in the organizations and communities you were part of? What problems do you want to have made smaller or solved? What generation of leaders do you want to have helped become? These are the questions your legacy statement answers.

The Ripple Effect of Your Leadership

Here is something that leadership development culture rarely acknowledges with enough clarity: your leadership does not stop with you. It ripples. Every person whose development you invest in goes on to influence others. Every culture you help shape influences the people who pass through it long after you have moved on. Every idea you champion, every standard you hold, every young leader you encourage, sends out concentric circles of influence that you will never be able to fully trace but that are nevertheless real and consequential.

I have been fortunate enough, across four decades, to watch some of those ripples return to me. A person I mentored twenty years ago who now leads a team of one hundred and still uses language I gave them. An organizational process I helped design that is still improving outcomes in an institution I left fifteen years ago. A young leader I believed in when others had not yet noticed them, who is now one of the most effective practitioners in their field. These are not trophies. They are evidence of a truth worth holding onto: when you lead well, the returns are not only personal. They compound across lives and institutions in ways that outlast any single role or moment.

This is the reason legacy matters now, not at the end of your career. Every day you lead with integrity, intentionality, and genuine care for the development of others is a day of compounding return. The ripples from good leadership are always bigger than they look from the center.

Investing in the Next Generation of Leaders

One of the most powerful legacy investments you can make is mentorship. Not as a formal program, not as an obligation, but as the genuine act of sharing what you know, what you have learned, and what you wish someone had told you, with a person who is navigating a path you have already walked.

Mentorship does not require superior expertise. It requires relevant experience and genuine commitment. The leader who is five years ahead of someone on a particular journey, who is willing to be honest about both their successes and their stumbles, who creates a relationship in which the mentee feels seen and challenged and supported simultaneously, can be transformative for that person's development in ways that formal education and training programs often cannot replicate.

If you have benefited from mentorship, you owe it forward. Not to the person who mentored you necessarily, but to someone who is where you were. That is how wisdom moves through generations of leaders. That is how the culture of a profession, an organization, a community, gradually improves over time. One honest, invested relationship at a time.

If you have not been formally mentored and you are reading this wondering how to mentor others without having experienced it yourself, the answer is simpler than you expect. Start with genuine curiosity about another person's development. Ask them what they are trying to build. Share what you have learned about the specific things they are navigating. Hold them to the commitments they make. Be honest when you see something they cannot see about themselves. That is mentorship. You already know how to do it.

The Leader You Are Becoming

This book began with a permission slip. An invitation to acknowledge that the leader you want to become is not some distant aspiration but a present reality that is already in development. I want to return to that invitation in this final chapter and make it as specific as possible.

You have, across these twelve chapters, done significant work. You have identified your FLEX personality style and begun understanding how your natural wiring shapes your leadership. You have mapped the five dimensions of your ALIGN Coaching Model blueprint and started developing each one with intentionality. You have walked through the Find, Learn, Empathize, and eXpand formula and begun applying it to your real leadership context. You have thought carefully about how you lead in school, work, home, and community. You have examined your relationship with failure and doubt and resilience. You have thought about legacy.

That is not trivial work. That is the kind of serious, reflective, honest self-examination that most people never do about their leadership, at any age, in any stage. The fact that you have done it, or are in the process of doing it, already distinguishes you from the majority of people who carry leadership potential without ever excavating it.

The leader you are becoming is not the leader you will be at the end of a career defined by accumulated titles and accomplishments. The leader you are becoming is the person who is one decision more honest, one conversation more courageous, one relationship more genuinely invested than you were when you began this book. That is not a small thing. Over a lifetime of leadership, those incremental improvements, consistently applied, become transformational.

Your Next Three Steps

I am not a believer in extended, elaborate action plans at the end of a book, because elaborate plans made in the afterglow of inspiration rarely survive contact with the complexity of real life. What I believe in is the next three concrete, specific, immediately actionable steps. Here are the ones I want you to take.

First: Complete the FLEX Style Assessment in Appendix A if you have not yet done so. Your instinct about your style from reading the descriptions in Chapter Two is a strong starting point, but the full assessment gives you the precision to work with your style at a more granular level. You can also complete it online at http://www.theflexleader.com/calculator.html .

Second: Choose one ALIGN dimension to focus on for the next ninety days. Just one. Use the Appendix C worksheets to build a specific, measurable development plan for that dimension. At the end of ninety days, assess your progress and choose the next dimension. This is not slow progress. This is sustainable progress, the kind that compounds.

Third: Tell someone that you have read this book and what you intend to change in your leadership because of it. Not because you need permission, but because accountability is one of the most powerful development accelerants available, and naming your intention to another person is the first act of the leader you are becoming.

YOUR LEGACY STATEMENT

Take ten minutes and write, in plain language, the answer to this question: When the people whose lives I have touched look back on the impact of my leadership, what do I most want them to be able to say? That is your legacy statement. Write it. Keep it somewhere visible. Lead toward it every day.

REFLECTION QUESTIONS

1. What is the most important insight from this book that you want to carry into your leadership practice immediately?

2. Who in your life is most likely to be directly impacted by the changes you make as a result of reading this book?

3. What commitment will you make to your own ongoing leadership development beyond this book?

4. Write your legacy statement. What do you most want to have contributed by the end of your leadership journey?

This area is for your thoughts:

IT'S NEVER TOO LATE TO LEAD: CONCLUSION
The Only Moment That Has Ever Mattered

You made it here.

I want to stop for a moment and let that land. Not as a formality, not as a congratulations for finishing a book, but as a genuine acknowledgment of something significant: you stayed. You showed up for the hard chapters. You sat with the reflection questions, even the ones that were uncomfortable. You read about your FLEX personality style and recognized yourself, the strengths and the growth edges both, without looking away. You did not skip the chapter on failure. You let the chapter on legacy sit with you.

That is not what everyone does. Most people start books. Significantly fewer finish them. And of the ones who finish, even fewer engage the material honestly, turning it on themselves, asking the real questions, and resisting the very human impulse to consume ideas without applying them.

If you are here, reading this conclusion, you are already in the smaller group. The one that does the work. And the work you have done in these pages, if you let it, will change the way you lead for the rest of your life.

Look at the Distance You Have Traveled

When you opened this book, you brought a question with you, even if you did not articulate it as a question. You brought the version of yourself that had doubts, gaps, and an honest uncertainty about whether the leadership you imagined for your life was still available to you.

You opened these pages as someone who may have believed, at some level, that leadership was a destination rather than a practice. That it required a particular kind of wiring you either had or did not have. That the window for becoming the leader you wanted to be might already have closed.

Look at what you know now.

You know your FLEX Personality Leadership Style. You know whether you are a Feeler who leads from the relational center, a Thinker who leads from analytical precision, a Controller who leads from results-driven momentum, or an Entertainer who leads from visionary energy. You know not just the name of your style but its specific signature strengths, its characteristic growth edges, and the ways it creates both natural advantages and predictable friction in your leadership relationships.

You know the ALIGN Coaching Model. You have the five-step framework that gives every leadership conversation structure and every coaching moment a clear path forward: Analyze Behaviors, Leverage Relationships, Inquire, Gain Next Steps, and New Commitment. You understand that this is not a script but a discipline, one that applied consistently turns ordinary feedback into lasting behavioral change, for the people you lead and for yourself.

You know the FLEX formula. You have walked through Find, Learn, Empathize, and eXpand not as abstract concepts but as practical leadership practices with specific applications in your specific context. You have thought about where you are, how you grow, how you see other people, and how you stretch beyond the limits of your current comfort and capability.

You have confronted the hard parts honestly. Failure. Doubt. The particular shape your imposter syndrome takes. The resilience foundations you need to build and maintain. The self-care you have been treating as optional when it is anything but.

And you have thought about legacy. About what you are building beyond yourself. About the ripples your leadership is already sending into the world. About the people who are watching how you handle difficulty, and learning from it. About the leader you are becoming, right now, in the small and unglamorous moments that actually determine who you are.

You have traveled a long way from the first page.

> *You did not find your leadership in this book. You found the language for what was already inside you. That is the most important discovery a leader ever makes.* *Shaine Hobdy, Author*

The Problem You Came With

You came to this book, directly or indirectly, because of a problem.

Maybe the problem had a name: a title you were passed over for, a team you were struggling to lead, a relationship that was fracturing under the weight of a style mismatch you could not diagnose, a transition you were navigating without the tools to navigate it well.

Maybe the problem was quieter than that. A sense of misalignment between the leader you knew you were capable of being and the leader your daily habits were actually producing. A vague but persistent feeling that your leadership was operating at half capacity, that something was being left on the table, that the gap between your potential and your practice was widening in a direction you did not want to accept.

Maybe the problem was the most quiet kind: the question. Is it too late for me? Is there still time? Has the window for becoming the leader I always imagined closed while I was busy surviving?

Whatever form the problem took when you arrived, I want to tell you what I believe with complete conviction after four decades in this field:

The problem was never a lack of talent. It was never a lack of ambition. It was never a lack of intelligence or character or desire. The problem was a lack of framework. You had the material. You needed the structure. And that is what this book was always designed to give you.

You have the structure now. The rest is practice.

THE TRANSFORMATION, STATED PLAINLY
You came to this book uncertain about your leadership. You are leaving it with a name for your style, a blueprint for your development, a formula for your growth, and the clearest answer you have ever received to the question that brought you here: it is not too late. It has never been too late. The leader you were always meant to be is the one you are becoming, right now, one intentional decision at a time.

The World That Is Waiting for Your Leadership

I want to say something that leadership books almost never say, because it requires a belief in you that most authors are too cautious to commit to in print.

The world needs your leadership specifically. Not just leadership in general. Not just good leadership from good people. Your leadership. The kind that only comes from your particular wiring, your particular history, your particular combination of FLEX style and hard-won wisdom and genuine care for the people around you.

There are people in your life right now, in your family, your school, your workplace, your community, who need the specific thing that you, as the specific leader you are becoming, uniquely provide. The Feeler whose relational intelligence will build the trust that makes a fractured team functional again. The Thinker whose analytical precision will catch the flaw in a plan that everyone else has already approved. The Controller whose clarity of expectation will finally give a drifting team the structure it has been starving for. The Entertainer whose vision will reignite people who have forgotten what they are working toward.

That is not a generic claim. It is a specific truth about specific people in specific situations who will be served or underserved depending on whether you choose to lead or choose to stay on the sideline of your own potential.

The sideline is no longer where you live. You have read this book. You have done this work. The sideline is behind you.

One More Honest Thing

I promised you at the beginning of this book that I would not waste your time with empty inspiration, and I intend to keep that promise all the way to the last sentence.

So here is the honest thing: finishing this book is not the finish line. It is the starting line. The clarity you have developed reading it is not the work of leadership. It is the preparation for the work. The real work happens Monday morning. It happens in the difficult conversation you have been putting off. It happens in the moment when your growth edge is tested by exactly the kind of situation that activates it. It happens when someone on your team needs the version of you that you have just been reading about, and you have to decide, in real time, whether you are going to lead from your best self or from your most defensive one.

Those moments are coming. They are always coming. And they will keep coming for as long as you choose to lead, which I hope and believe will be for the rest of your life.

What will be different now is that you will have something you did not have before those moments arrive: a framework for understanding what is happening, a language for what you are feeling, a model for the decision you need to make, and the knowledge, earned through the honest self-examination of these pages, that you are capable of making it well.

That is not a small gift. That is the whole point.

Your Next Step Starts in the Next Five Minutes

I am not going to send you away with a list of things to do someday. Here is what I want you to do today, before you put this book down, before you get back to the inbox and the to-do list and the real world that is already pulling at your attention.

Do one thing.

Not five things. Not a ninety-day leadership plan. One thing. The most important next thing, the one this book has been pointing you toward, the action that sits at the intersection of your FLEX Personality style, your most urgent ALIGN dimension, and the leadership challenge that is most alive for you right now.

Maybe that thing is a conversation you have been avoiding. Maybe it is the FLEX Personality Style Assessment in Appendix A, finally completed with the honesty it deserves. Maybe it is a message to the person who should be mentoring you, finally sent. Maybe it is writing your legacy statement in the margin of the last page of Appendix C. Maybe it is simply telling someone, out loud, about the leader you are committed to becoming.

Whatever that one thing is, do it today. Not because momentum requires it, though it does. Not because the habits of change are formed in the earliest moments, though they are. But because the version of you that does that one thing today is already, in that single act, different from the version of you that began this book.

And different, in this direction, is everything.

> *The leadership that changes the world is never delivered by someone who had no doubt. It is delivered by someone who had every doubt — and led anyway. – Shaine Hobdy, Author*

IT'S NEVER TOO LATE TO LEAD.

Not tomorrow. Not after the next promotion. Not after the doubt is gone.

Now. Today. In this moment. With everything you already are.

— *Shaine Hobdy*

https://www.flexleadershipsystem.com

APPENDIX A: The FLEX Personality Style Assessment
Discover Your Dominant Leadership Style

The FLEX Personality Style Assessment is a self-report instrument designed to identify your dominant leadership personality style across the four FLEX dimensions: Feeler, Thinker, Controller, and Entertainer.

The online FLEX Personality Calculator is available at this link in English and Spanish: https://www.flexpersonality.com

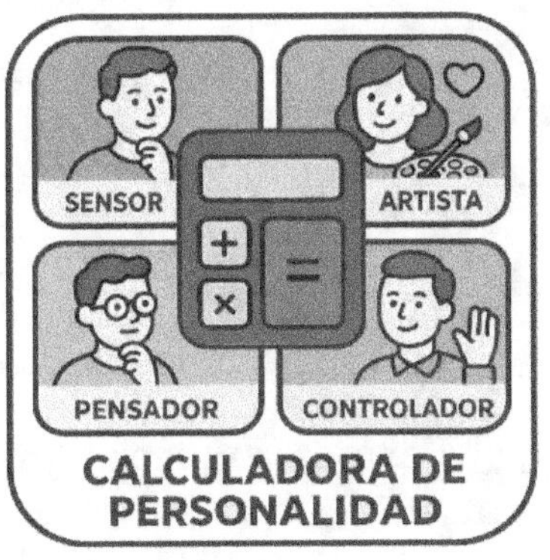

In the next few pages, rate how strongly each statement describes you by selecting the score from the scoring guide. Your responses will help identify how much you naturally align with this communication style. DON'T OVER THINK IT! JUST SELECT YOUR FIRST RESPONSE & ANSWER THEM NATURALLY.

Read each statement and assign a score from 1 to 5 based on how accurately it describes you:

SCORING GUIDE
1 = Rarely or never describes me
2 = Sometimes describes me
3 = Often describes me
4 = Almost always describes me
5 = Always describes me

SECTION 1:

_______I easily pick up on other people's emotions

_______I care deeply about how people feel.

_______I take it personally when someone is upset with me.

_______I try to avoid conflict whenever possible.

_______I want people to feel included.

_______I worry about hurting someone's feelings.

_______I value harmony in groups.

_______I express appreciation often.

_______I try to make people comfortable in conversations.

Section 1 TOTAL: _______

Shaine Hobdy

Read each statement and assign a score from 1 to 5 based on how accurately it describes you:

SCORING GUIDE
1 = Rarely or never describes me
2 = Sometimes describes me
3 = Often describes me
4 = Almost always describes me
5 = Always describes me

SECTION 2:

_______I like to understand the facts before I respond.

_______I often analyze situations logically.

_______I prefer clear, detailed instructions.

_______I notice inconsistencies quickly.

_______I take time to think before making decisions.

_______I ask questions to understand the reasoning behind things.

_______I stay calm when others get emotional.

_______I like step-by-step plans.

_______I trust logic more than emotion.

_______I value accuracy in communication.

Section 2 TOTAL: _______

Read each statement and assign a score from 1 to 5 based on how accurately it describes you:

SCORING GUIDE
1 = Rarely or never describes me
2 = Sometimes describes me
3 = Often describes me
4 = Almost always describes me
5 = Always describes me

SECTION 3:

_______I like taking charge in group situations.

_______I want decisions made quickly.

_______I get frustrated when things move slowly.

_______I prefer direct communication.

_______I focus on results over emotions.

_______I naturally step up to lead when things are unclear.

_______I feel more comfortable when I'm in control.

_______I prefer clear, actionable steps.

_______I get impatient with indecision.

_______I like to solve problems quickly.

Section 3 TOTAL: _______

Shaine Hobdy

Read each statement and assign a score from 1 to 5 based on how accurately it describes you:

SCORING GUIDE
1 = Rarely or never describes me
2 = Sometimes describes me
3 = Often describes me
4 = Almost always describes me
5 = Always describes me

SECTION 4:

_______I bring energy into conversations.

_______I like making people laugh or feel at ease.

_______I enjoy being expressive when I talk.

_______I like conversations to feel upbeat and fun.

_______I get bored when things feel slow.

_______I'm good at getting others engaged.

_______I enjoy being spontaneous.

_______I prefer variety over routine.

_______I like coming up with creative ideas.

_______I notice when a room needs more energy.

Section 4 TOTAL: _______

INTERPRETING YOUR RESULTS

Transfer your four section totals here:

Section 1 Total (Feeler): _________

Section 2 Total (Thinker): _________

Section 3 Total (Controller): _________

Section 4 Total (Entertainer): _________

Your highest score is your Dominant FLEX Style. A score of 40 or above indicates a strong orientation toward that style.

Your second-highest score is your Secondary Style, which influences how your dominant style expresses itself in different contexts.

If two scores are within 3 points of each other, both styles are active in your leadership wiring. Read both descriptions and pay particular attention to the growth edges of each.

APPENDIX B: Chapter Journaling Prompts
A Deeper Practice for Every Chapter

The reflection questions at the end of each chapter are designed to be engaged in the moment. These extended journaling prompts are designed for deeper, more sustained reflection. Return to them regularly, especially during leadership transitions.

Introduction: The Permission Slip

Write about a moment when you did not give yourself permission to lead. What was the cost of that decision? What would you say to the version of yourself in that moment?

Chapter 1: What Is a Leader, Really?

Describe the most influential informal leader you have personally known. What specifically made them effective? How does their leadership challenge or expand your definition of leadership?

Chapter 2: Meet Your FLEX Personality Style

Write a letter from your dominant FLEX style to your growth edge. What would your natural strengths say to the areas of your leadership that need development?

Chapter 3: The ALIGN Coaching Model

Which of the five ALIGN steps do you find most difficult to practice honestly: Analyze Behaviors, Leverage Relationships, Inquire, Gain Next Steps, or New Commitment? Write about a specific leadership situation in which skipping that step created a measurable cost.

Chapter 4: Strengths Are Your Starting Line

Describe a time when you were operating fully from your strengths. What was the context? What specifically did you do? What were the results? What would it take to create more moments like that one?

Chapter 5: <u>F</u>ind

Conduct a full leadership position audit using the four dimensions: influence currency, skill-gap map, energy audit, and relationship landscape. Write about what you found in each one.

Chapter 6: <u>L</u>earn

Name the three most significant leadership lessons of your life so far. For each one, write: what the experience was, what you extracted from it, and how you have applied what you learned.

Chapter 7: <u>E</u>mpathize

Choose one person in your leadership life whose inner experience you do not fully understand. Write from their perspective about what it is like to be led by you. What do you discover?

Chapter 8: e**X**pand

What is the most significant growth you have ever experienced in your leadership? What made it possible? What resisted it? What would have made it happen faster?

Chapter 9: Leading Across Styles

Describe your most challenging cross-style relationship in detail. Using what you now know about FLEX, reinterpret that person's behavior through their style lens. How does that reinterpretation change your approach?

Chapter 10: Leading in Real Life

Evaluate your leadership consistency across all four contexts: school or educational settings, work, home, and community. Where is the gap widest between who you are in one context and who you are in another?

Chapter 11: When Leadership Gets Hard

Write honestly about your greatest leadership failure to date. Use the Learning Loop from Chapter Six to fully process it: What happened? What is your reflection? What is the specific insight? What is your application going forward?

Chapter 12 & Conclusion

Write your complete leadership legacy statement. Make it specific, personal, and grounded in your FLEX personality style and the ALIGN Coaching Model blueprint. Then write a letter to the leader you will be ten years from now. What do you want them to know about where you are starting?

APPENDIX C: ALIGN Coaching Worksheets
Your Personal Leadership Blueprint

The following worksheets apply the five steps of the ALIGN Coaching Model to your own leadership development. Work through each one honestly. Revisit them quarterly. Share them with a mentor or accountability partner who will hold you to what you discover.

WORKSHEET 1: A — <u>Analyze Behaviors</u>

WHAT TO DO: Gather honest data about your own leadership behaviors the way a coach would gather data about a team member. Look for patterns, not isolated incidents.

My dominant FLEX Style is: _______________________________________

My secondary FLEX Style is: ______________________________________

Three behavioral patterns I consistently observe in my leadership (positive):

1. ____

2. ____

3. ____

Three behavioral patterns I consistently observe in my leadership (growth areas):

1. ____

2. ____

3. ____

Three words others consistently use to describe my leadership:

1. ____

2. ____

3. ____

Three words I wish others used to describe my leadership:

1. ____

2. ____

3. ____

The pattern that is costing me most right now:

____

____

The data source I have been avoiding (feedback, metrics, honest conversation):

____

____

____

____

WORKSHEET 2: L — <u>L</u>everage Relationships

WHAT TO DO: Map the key relationships in your leadership life. Identify where trust is strong, where it needs investment, and what specifically you will do to build it.

The five most important leadership relationships in my current context:

1. _________________________________ Trust level (1–10): ______
Last meaningful check-in: _____________________

2. _________________________________ Trust level (1–10): ______
Last meaningful check-in: _____________________

3. _________________________________ Trust level (1–10): ______
Last meaningful check-in: _____________________

4. _________________________________ Trust level (1–10): ______
Last meaningful check-in: _____________________

5. _________________________________ Trust level (1–10): ______
Last meaningful check-in: _____________________

The relationship where the trust deficit is most affecting outcomes: _______________________________________

____

What created the deficit: _____________________________

____

____

One specific action I will take in the next 14 days to invest in that relationship: ____

____

The relationship I most consistently take for granted: _________

____

How I will show that relationship more intentional care this month: ____

____

____

WORKSHEET 3: I — <u>Inquire</u>

WHAT TO DO: Apply the ALIGN Inquire framework to yourself. Use the Who, What, Where, When, and Why questions to investigate the root cause of your most persistent leadership challenge.

The leadership behavior or pattern I am investigating: __________

____

____

WHO is involved or affected by this pattern? ______________

____

____

WHAT specifically happens? (Describe the observable behavior, not the interpretation.) __________________________

____

____

WHERE does this pattern most consistently occur? __________

____

____

WHEN does it occur? (What conditions, pressures, or triggers precede it?) __________________________

____

____

WHY does it happen? (First answer): _______________________
____

WHY does that happen? (Go deeper): _____________________

____

____

WHY does THAT happen? (Root cause): ___________________

____
____
____

The real root cause, beneath the surface explanation, is: _______

____

____

____

WORKSHEET 4: G — <u>G</u>ain Next Steps

WHAT TO DO: Using the root cause identified in Worksheet 3, co-create a concrete, SMART action plan with yourself. Every Next Step must be Specific, Measurable, Achievable, Relevant, and Time-bound.

The behavioral change I am committing to: _________________

____

____

NEXT STEP 1:

What I will do: _______________________________

By when: ___________________

How I will measure success: ____________________

____

NEXT STEP 2:

What I will do: _______________________________

By when: ___________________

How I will measure success: ____________________

____

NEXT STEP 3:

What I will do: _______________________________

By when: ___________________

How I will measure success: ____________________

____

Resources or support I need to execute these steps: _______________

____

____

____

Obstacles I anticipate and how I will address them: _______________

____

____

____

WORKSHEET 5: N — <u>New Commitment</u>

WHAT TO DO: Make your commitment explicit, assign an accountability partner, and schedule your follow-up. A Next Step without a New Commitment is just an intention. This step is what makes it real.

My complete commitment statement (write it in full, in your own words):

I commit to ____

____

____

by ____________________________ (date), because ________________

____

____

My accountability partner (name someone who will check in on this commitment): ____________________________________

Date I will share this commitment with them: ________________

Date of my first follow-up check-in: ____________________________

Date of my 30-day review: ______________________________________

Date of my 90-day review: ______________________________________

What I will look for as evidence that my commitment is producing real behavioral change: ______________________

____

____

____

If I fall short of this commitment, here is how I will respond rather than abandon it: ______________________

____

THE ALIGN COACHING ROADMAP

Use these five worksheets together as your personal ALIGN Coaching Roadmap. Begin with Analyze. Let each step inform the next. Return to the beginning whenever a new leadership challenge emerges or whenever a quarterly review reveals that the pattern you addressed has evolved into a new one.

The ALIGN Coaching Model is not a one-time exercise. It is a lifelong practice of honest self-coaching that becomes more precise and more powerful every time you use it.

APPENDIX D: Find Step - Four Dimensions

Find Step - Dimension 1: Your Influence Currency

Memory Hook	Trust Account
Simple Picture	Think of leadership trust like a bank account. Every conversation affects the balance.
What It Means	How much credibility, trust, and relational capital do you currently hold with the people you are leading? Every interaction either makes a deposit into that account or a withdrawal from it.
What to Notice	Notice where your account feels full and where it feels low. This dimension helps you assess whether people are already inclined to follow your lead or whether trust needs to be rebuilt first.
Reflection Questions	Where is trust already strong? Where is your credibility low or uncertain? What recent interactions added to the account? What recent interactions may have withdrawn from it?

Use this page as a quick appendix reference before moving into action.

Find Step - Dimension 2: Your Skill-Gap Map

Memory Hook	Target the Gap
Simple Picture	Do not label a foggy weakness. Identify a specific leadership skill you can develop.
What It Means	What does your current context require of you that you are not yet fully developed in? The goal is to name the gap specifically enough that you can work on it.
What to Notice	Avoid vague statements such as 'be more confident.' Name the exact behavior or conversation skill you need, such as delivering a performance conversation without damaging the relationship.
Reflection Questions	What is this season of leadership asking from you? Which skill is missing or underdeveloped? Can you describe the gap in one specific sentence? What would stronger performance look like in action?

Use this page as a quick appendix reference before moving into action.

Find Step - Dimension 3: Your Energy Audit

Memory Hook	Follow the Return
Simple Picture	Track where your leadership energy goes. Then compare it with where your best contribution belongs.
What It Means	Where are you spending your leadership energy, and is that where your energy produces the most return? Track your time for one week without editing it, then compare it to your highest-value contribution.
What to Notice	This dimension reveals whether your effort is being spent on low-return activity or on the work that only you can do well. Leadership energy should be aligned with impact, not just urgency.
Reflection Questions	Where did your time actually go this week? What activities drained energy without meaningful return? Where does your highest-value contribution truly lie? What should receive more of your focused attention?

Use this page as a quick appendix reference before moving into action.

Find Step - Dimension 4: Your Relationship Landscape

Memory Hook	Map the Tension
Simple Picture	Draw the map of your most important relationships so you can see where trust needs attention.
What It Means	Map your five most important current leadership relationships. For each one, ask whether there is trust or tension, honest communication or things left unsaid, and what it would take to strengthen the relationship.
What to Notice	This dimension helps you see the relational terrain around you. Strong leadership rarely happens in isolation. It rises or falls through the health of your key relationships.
Reflection Questions	Who are your five most important leadership relationships right now? Where is there trust, and where is there tension? What has been left unsaid? What would strengthen each relationship?

Use this page as a quick appendix reference before moving into action.

APPENDIX E: Learn – The Learning Loop

THE LEARNING LOOP

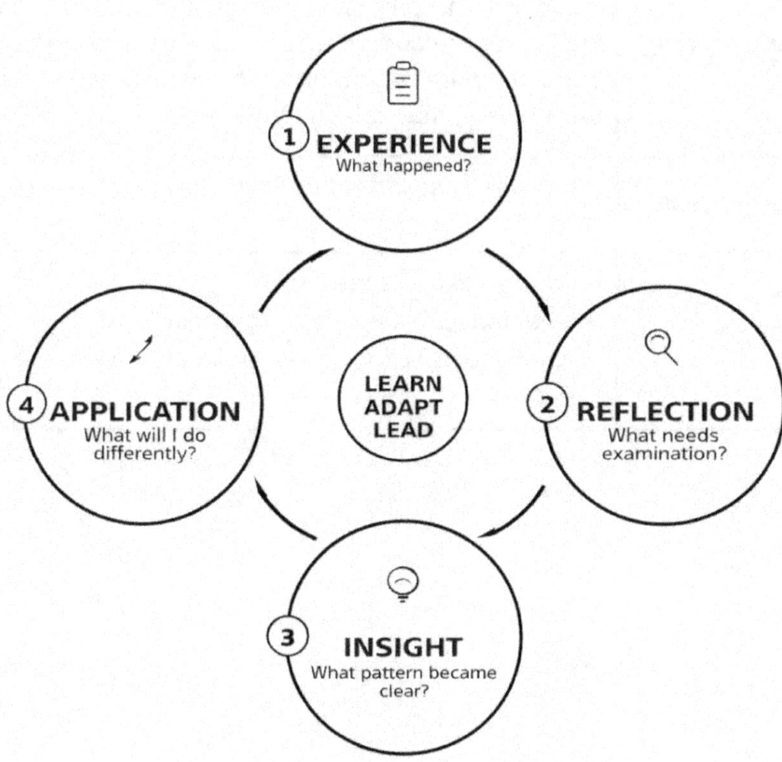

1 Experience → 2 Reflection → 3 Insight
4 Application → Repeat

The Learning Loop – Stage One: The Experience

STAGE ONE	**The Experience** RAW MATERIAL
WHAT IT IS	This is the event itself - the meeting that went sideways, the project that collapsed under its own weight, or the conversation that revealed a gap you did not know you had. The experience is just the raw material. It is not yet learning.
QUESTIONS	*Use these questions to move the experience into learning.*
TRY THIS	• What actually happened? • What made this moment significant? • What gap, reaction, or result did the experience expose?

The Learning Loop – Stage Two: Reflection

STAGE TWO	**Reflection** **EXAMINE IT**
WHAT IT IS	This is where most learning opportunities die. After the experience, the urgent pulls you back into action - and the experience, with all of its embedded learning, goes unexamined and therefore unretrieved. Effective reflection is honest without being punishing. It is curious without being defensive. It asks why the team responded that way to your approach, what signal you missed early in the conversation, and what assumption turned out to be inaccurate.
QUESTIONS	*Use these questions to move the experience into learning.*
TRY THIS	• Why did people respond the way they did? • What did I miss, assume, or overlook? • What would an honest reading of my role reveal?

The Learning Loop – Stage Three: Insight

STAGE THREE	**Insight** **SEE THE PATTERN**
WHAT IT IS	Insight is what emerges from sustained, honest reflection - the moment when the pattern becomes visible, when you understand something about yourself that you did not understand before. The quality of your insights depends entirely on the quality of your reflection questions. Shallow questions produce shallow insights.
QUESTIONS	*Use these questions to move the experience into learning.*
TRY THIS	• What pattern is becoming visible? • What am I learning about myself, my leadership, or this situation? • What truth do I need to name clearly?

The Learning Loop – Stage Four: Application

STAGE FOUR	**Application** **DO IT DIFFERENTLY**
WHAT IT IS	This is where learning becomes leadership. Without it, the first three stages are simply interesting self-examination that produces no behavioral change. Application means you take the insight you have developed - and you do something different the next time. That is it. That is the whole thing. Something different.
QUESTIONS	*Use these questions to move the experience into learning.*
TRY THIS	• What will I do differently next time? • What behavior, response, or decision will change? • How will I know the learning has been applied?

APPENDIX F: Empathize – Empathetic Leadership

EMPATHETIC LEADERSHIP

LEVEL ONE

Situational Awareness

Read the room. Notice who is engaged, who is checked out, and whose energy has shifted.

Leadership practice
- Observe patterns
- Ask questions
- Stay present

LEVEL TWO

Perspective-Taking

Set aside your own frame long enough to understand another person's experience from the inside.

Leadership practice
- Pause your lens
- Consider their context
- Ask what this means to them

LEVEL THREE

Empathetic Response

Respond to what you observed and understood in a way that genuinely serves the other person.

Leadership practice
- Support
- Challenge
- Set clear expectations

APPENDIX G: eXpand – Expansion Growth Zone

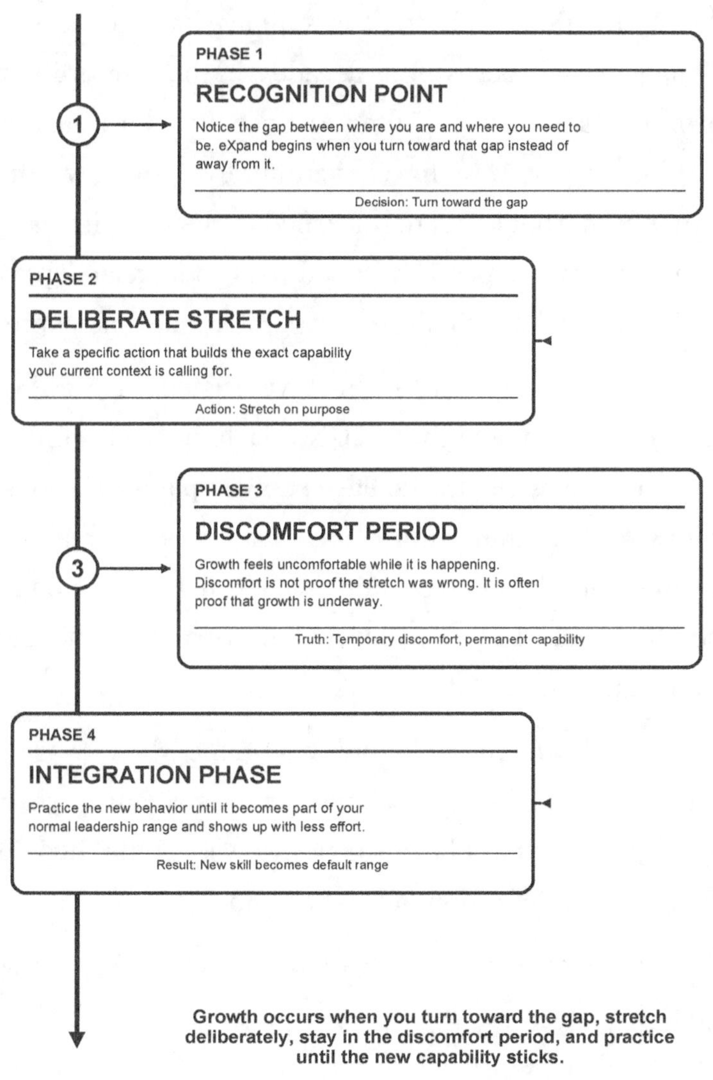

ACKNOWLEDGMENTS: With Gratitude

Every book is a collaboration, even the ones with a single name on the cover. This one is no exception.

To the thousands of leaders, I have had the privilege of working alongside across four decades, in the extraordinary environments of Disney, United Airlines, Ritz-Carlton, Asurion, and Assurant, you were the curriculum. Everything worth knowing in this book was first learned in the field, in real moments, from real people who led with courage and grace and, sometimes, instructive failure. I am grateful beyond expression.

To the young leaders who have trusted the FLEX Leadership System and the ALIGN Coaching Model frameworks with their development, who have shown up to workshops and coaching sessions and lecture halls ready to do the real work of knowing themselves and building something better, you are the reason this book exists. Your growth is not a byproduct of this work. It is the point of it.

To every mentor who invested in me when I was not yet who I would become, your belief was infrastructure. You built something in me that I have spent forty years building in others. That is the best definition of legacy I know.

To the readers of this book: thank you for choosing growth. Thank you for taking leadership seriously. Thank you for the courage it takes to look honestly at yourself and decide that the leader you want to be is worth becoming. It is. You are.

Shaine Hobdy

The world does not have too many leaders. It has too many people who have not yet discovered theirs. This book was written for the ones who are ready to discover.

Lead forward.

9 798999 924729